2001

BECAUSE WE ARE AMERICANS

Because We Are Americans

WHAT WE DISCOVERED ON SEPTEMBER 11, 2001

EDITED BY

JESSE KORNBLUTH AND JESSICA PAPIN

AMERICA *Online.*

WARNER BOOKS

An AOL Time Warner Company

Cover design by Christopher Standish
Book design by Jaime Putorti

For information address Warner Books, 1271 Avenue of the Americas, New York, NY 10020.

 An AOL Time Warner Company

ISBN 0-446-61198-0

First edition: November 2001

Visit our website at twbookmark.com

Printed in the United States of America

10 9 8 7 6 5 4 3 2 1

CONTENTS

INTRODUCTION

On the morning of September 11 it was warm and clear in New York City, with just a hint of fall in the air. Going to work on days like that, you think how good life is, and you contemplate taking a stroll at lunch, walking home through the park, or heading out to a baseball stadium in the cool of the evening to catch one of our pennant contenders play in a game that really matters.

But as I stepped off a downtown bus at 8:50 A.M., all those pleasant thoughts vanished. For in America's busiest city, with the workday just beginning, people were standing around, looking up at a thick stream of dark smoke.

"A plane hit the World Trade Center," someone said.

There was no panic, just puzzlement: How *does*

a plane, on a sparkling day, crash into a skyscraper so tall you can see it for miles? Something felt wrong. I hurried upstairs, logged on to America Online and turned on CNN.

Minutes later, I watched a jetliner zoom across the television screen and explode as it crashed into the Trade Center's second tower.

The next thing I clearly remember was that my computer screen was filled with Instant Messages. The ones from friends were urgent and personal: "I'm okay. Are you?" The ones from AOL colleagues in other buildings asked the same question. Then, like people who work in media all across America, we moved quickly beyond our own reactions to practicality: "Let's get to work."

And so, minutes after the second plane hit the Trade Center, with two other hijacked planes still hurtling toward their targets, AOL set about reporting the awful events.

Updating the news—and throwing cold water on the rumors that raced across America—was only the start of the ways that AOL and other online services helped hold our country together that day and in the days to come. After all, news was available around the clock on radio and television, on many Web sites, and in special editions of big-city newspapers. And those sources did a terrific job in helping us comprehend the day's impossible-to-understand events.

What online services and some Web sites offered, in addition to news, was something just as important and maybe more so: the chance to reach out and talk with a world of people who were at once distant strangers and immediate friends.

On a normal day, most of us don't think of the technological miracle called "interactivity" as anything extraordinary. We read and send e-mail as if we've been doing it forever, even though for most of us it's only been a few years. Teenagers who have scores of friends on their Buddy Lists come home from school and send Instant Messages to kids they saw just a few minutes ago, and everyone accepts that as part of the fabric of day-to-day life. It took September 11 to demonstrate what the ability to "find" people online can mean in times of crisis.

Terrorism is unlike other forms of war—its primary targets are civilians. And the point of terrorist attacks isn't just to kill or wound the innocent; it's also to break the opponent's will to fight back. So hijacking jets and crashing them into buildings was only a prelude; the real detonations were to occur in the psyches of the American people, who were supposed to feel isolated and defenseless, betrayed by our country's inadequate security—and horribly alone.

But when we went online that day, we weren't alone. We reached out for friends and loved ones, only to discover that many of our friends and loved ones were going online to reach out for us. And then, once the overwhelming majority of us saw that our friends and loved ones were alive, we reached out to the larger online community.

In New York City, telephone service was disrupted by the attack; land lines didn't work well, and even cellular service was spotty. People quickly discovered that online services were often the simplest way to communicate. Like my friends and colleagues, they began with Instant Messages; just on AOL, 1.2 *billion* were sent that day. They followed up with message board postings that, like the Instant Messages, had a common theme: "Have you seen . . . ?" Then, as the impossible fact of a terrorist assault on America began to sink in, people shared their fears and consoled one another.

At America Online, experts on terrorism and trauma streamed into virtual auditoriums—which remained open and staffed around the clock—and gave us advice about talking to our children and dealing with our own distress.

Every online service and hundreds of Web sites began publishing contact information for the Red Cross and other charities.

In days to come, "normal" process was forgotten. At AOL, and, I'm sure, at other online services and Web sites, people worked around the clock—we all understood that interactive media was Ground Zero of the American conversation about the attack and its aftermath. Special features sprouted everywhere: poems from teenagers, drawings from children, tributes to the dead and missing.

And it didn't ebb. At AOL, numbers told us how important time online was to a hurting nation: unprecedented participation in AOL Live events, tens of thousands of message board posts, millions of votes in our polls, and millions of dollars donated. But even more meaningful was the shift—from confusion to resolve, from grief to inspiration—you could chart in the chats and on the boards.

That resilience is not limited to Americans; around the world, people triumph over circumstance. But there is something thrillingly American about 285,000,000 people getting knocked down, mourning their losses, and then dusting themselves off and setting out to rebuild. If how we behaved in our communities and online during those few weeks in September is any guide, the American spirit will be a greater challenge than any the terrorists have ever faced.

This book is a record of that transformation from shock and grief to resolve and rededication. For those who were online during those long days and endless nights, it's a reminder of the stages we passed through; for those who weren't online, the chronicle of reactions you'll find here probably mirrors the reactions you experienced in your community. And, to give us a sense of perspective, we've included comments and wisdom from some of America's greatest leaders and thinkers, from crises past to this latest trial.

It's been hard for all of us since September 11. Two cities we love are crippled, and many, many others have suffered grievous losses. There are too many people on our Buddy Lists who aren't around anymore. And the ripple effect of loss and grief sneaks up on us, as, we suspect, it sneaks up on you. But we have been freshly inspired as we have worked on this book. We hope you will find inspiration here too.

Jesse Kornbluth
Editorial Director, America Online

CONNECTED

FROM AN AOL NEWSROOM CHAT, 9/11/2001
9:45 AM EASTERN DAYLIGHT TIME

AOL HOST: This is what we know so far: Two planes crashed into the World Trade Center in New York City. Another hit the Pentagon. The White House and Pentagon have been evacuated.

QUESTION: How many people were hurt?

AOL HOST: Not known. But it does appear that one plane was an American Airlines 767 hijacked from Boston shortly after takeoff. I can only think that plane had 100+ people on it.

QUESTION: Who do you think is responsible for this?

AOL HOST: "Terrorists" is too vague, but it's the best we can say right now.

QUESTION: I want to know what they are going to do about the military.

AOL HOST: I would say that we are on full military alert.

QUESTION: Is the White House on fire?

AOL HOST: No. There is a fire at the Pentagon, where a plane seems to have crashed.

QUESTION: Who has claimed responsibility for these acts of terrorism?

AOL HOST: No one. And that is very nervous-making, don't you think?

QUESTION: Would you speculate on responsibility? They keep saying Palestinians, but this is more like Iraq, considering the recent plane downings near Baran.

AOL HOST: I hear you, but I think it's best not to speculate just yet.

QUESTION: Will this lead to a war?

AOL HOST: If so, it is a different kind of war than we usually fight.

QUESTION: Is there any reason to believe that the terrorists will attack the White House?

AOL HOST: If so, I think it would have happened already. But we do not know if there are other planes in the air.

QUESTION: Do you know what hit the Pentagon?

AOL HOST: No.

QUESTION: Why weren't the planes detected by radar?

AOL HOST: Good question. And here is another: If one of the planes was hijacked from Boston, was the government tracking it for almost an hour?

QUESTION: What does this say about the apparent inadequate security at a major airport?

AOL HOST: It says there is no such thing as "security."

NEWSFLASH: One of the World Trade Center towers just collapsed. Now let us recap. A plane hit near or at the Pentagon. Two planes crashed into the World Trade Center. The president is on his way back to D.C. All airports in U.S. closed. Unclear how many dead . . . There are many rumors, but that is all they are—rumors. We'll confirm them as they're authenticated—IF they are authenticated. New York City is completely closed: bridges and subways and tunnels. And airports are closed. We have lots of anecdotal reports that many, many people have been terrific in helping others out of the buildings and out of the area . . .

"Hi, Mom . . . I love you very much. I'm calling you from the plane. We've been taken over."

—MARK BINGHAM, TO HIS MOTHER IN
SAN FRANCISCO, *Newsday* 9/13/2001

※

"People jumped online and they IM'd me and said, 'Are you okay? Is your brother okay? Do you know anybody who's missing?'"

—HOST OF A SMALL WEB JOURNAL,
Entertainment Weekly 9/28/2001

※

FROM AN AOL POST, 9/12/2001 12:18 PM
EASTERN DAYLIGHT TIME
SUBJECT WHERE WERE YOU WHEN THE
TOWERS CAME DOWN?

I was breast-feeding my three-month-old son and crying. What kind of world did I bring my son into, and will he ever be safe? Will he have to witness to such a catastrophic tragedy? I pray to God that he will not.

※

FROM AN AOL POST, 9/14/2001 5:04 AM
EASTERN DAYLIGHT TIME
SUBJECT: EVERY TIME I HEAR A PLANE I
          CRINGE

Last night, 9/13/01, all flights were canceled at JFK, LaGuardia, and, Newark.

About 9:30 PM I heard a plane, and my body froze, waiting to see the news of another target hit. Fifteen minutes later I heard another one. Again, I froze.

I realized from the first plane that they are military aircraft patrolling our air space, but I think I'd be happy if I never heard the roar of a jet engine again in my life. I live in the Bronx and in the flight paths to the various airports, and I feel like I'm holding my breath, just waiting for the other shoe to drop. I know I should feel safe with all the military protection (aircraft carriers, etc.), but I just can't seem to take a completely deep breath.

I am 40 years old. I went from the Garden of Eden to hell. I am afraid for my family. Is nerve gas next on the list of terrorist deeds?

I am afraid for my country. Is our economic way of life doomed?

I am afraid for my world. Is this the beginning of the end for mankind? I feel I have no control over my world anymore. Help me—the depression is really deep. The terrorist bastards have won, and the images of the WTC falling haunt me day and night.

*

I felt such fear when I first learned about these horrific attacks on our peace and way of life. I felt exactly as you described. Being 51 years old, I've been through some nasty episodes in my lifetime, enough to have learned that "feeling better is a do-it-yourself project."

I know that if I'm going to feel safe again, I'm the one who's going to have to take the steps to feel that way. Me. Not the government, not the terrorists, not Mommy and Daddy. Me. So I decided that I would help myself to feel safe again.

The first thing I did was to limit my exposure to it, so I've watched the latest developments just once a day. I'm not sticking my head in the sand, but I'm not sticking it out there for the media to shoot off either!

Another thing I've done is made the decision to trust our country's leaders and a loving "higher power." I'm scheduled to fly from Boston to San Francisco in January, and I will go. I'm uncomfortable with that, but I'm going. I decide to trust.

One of the things that helped me feel safer is realizing that I AM safer. Really. We are all safer today than we were a week ago! Physically safer. It's safer to fly today because of all the precautions now being taken. And if I felt safe last week, I can feel safe this week.

I just FEEL more vulnerable. This is just a feeling, not a fact, and it need not govern my life. On the other hand, feeling a realistic amount of vulnerability is a good thing. It can lead one to pursue one's own truth, and it can motivate us to live fully and treasure each day.

There are many ways to experience the events of the past week. I'm quite sure we all experienced the same initial emotional response—great fear and sadness and anger. But we can choose not to be stuck in that place, not to live there. We can CHOOSE "life, liberty and the pursuit of happiness."

I don't have control over the world—I never did! I do have control over MY internal world, and really, that's the world I inhabit. The "terrorist bastards" can only win if I lay down and let them win. My choosing to feel safe, choosing to go on with my life just as I've planned—including the cross-country flight—this is what keeps them from winning.

Yes, I have some fear, but I also have a lot of trust. I am saddened by the scenes of devastation and loss, but also encouraged by the scenes of human love and kindness and patriotism. I believe that feeling our vulnerability makes us stronger, wiser and more loving.

And I choose to focus on the positive.

I am 54, and I too, went from the garden into hell. I am afraid of all the same things, too. This world should be such a wonderful place—a celebration of the diversity of people and beliefs, and all of the wonderful choices we should be able to make for our lives.

I am beginning to pull myself out of fear and depression this way: I am telling ALL of the people I love and care for how I feel about them and the difference they have made in my life.

I look back on my life, all of the mistakes that I have made and all of the wonderful things I have done and become, and I am proud and satisfied.

I look forward to what I can do to spread kindness every day in every way that I can, to all sorts of people.

I look at my ethnically different neighbors with a mixture of mistrust and concern for their safety as Americans like me and as intrinsically good people, knowing that the terrorists have disguised themselves as these same good families. I struggle not to fall into that destructive, suspicious mindset. While I struggle, I smile and practice kindness.

I know we must fight, and I believe many will die, probably horribly, and probably right here at home, in our neighborhoods, maybe even in my house. When I am most troubled by these thoughts, I think that everything has its time and life is transitory anyway. We know we all will die. It's how we live that matters.

You have my appreciation for sharing your feelings . . . your thoughts have helped me come to a better place within myself.

*

"The Internet carries the news and connects the masses in a true interactive sob."

—DONNA HOFFMAN, A PROFESSOR AT VAN-DERBILT UNIVERSITY WHO STUDIES THE WEB, *The New York Times* 9/12/2001

*

My husband and I have been mourning right along with the rest of the nation since Tuesday morning. Before this I'd only seen my husband cry one other time—the day our son was born. But seeing the destruction and listening to the personal stories of the victims and their families had him crying right alongside me.

I am writing in this forum because I have to be scared now for a whole different reason than most Americans. Not only do I worry about the threat of war, but now I am also scared of my fellow American. I fear my fellow American. God, isn't it so sad that anyone should have to say that?

I am not scared for myself. I am the kind of "American" who is generally accepted and not singled out. I'm just your average white girl. I've lived the great majority of my life without the eye of prejudice looking upon me—but it is now focused on my husband and son.

My husband's name is Marwan and our son is Khaled. Clearly not your typical American names, but they are certainly Americans. Just as much as you or I. Marwan's mother is just another white girl like me, but his father is Palestinian. Marwan is an American citizen by birth and grew up right alongside all of us. He cheered at college football games. He said the Pledge of Allegiance every day in school. He was horrified when the Space Shuttle Challenger exploded. He was president of his college fraternity. He was a band geek, and now is a computer geek. He has that same love/hate relationship with 80s music that all of our generation shares. He gives blood every year—not just when there's a tragedy. He votes. That sounds pretty "American," doesn't it? He knows no other culture—this IS his land.

So why on earth would people start telling him to "go home" now? He IS home, damn it. His home is right in the United States of America with his wife and baby boy.

Three nights ago a man told me, anonymously by computer like a true coward, that my son's "blood is poisoned" and that my husband is an "Arab pig." Have we not learned anything from this? Please someone tell me that from this tragedy people will learn and see what comes from anger and hatred. At a time when we should all be coming together, why would we be turning against each other? And why would we start to blame innocent people?

If my husband were to trade his baseball cap and blue jeans for traditional Middle Eastern attire, would that make him less American? No. If he were to trade the Bible for the Koran, would it make him less American? No. Then why would anyone want to fire-bomb mosques? Why would someone make death threats to Islamic school-children?

I am tired of crying myself to sleep. I am tired of being afraid every time my husband walks out the door. I am angry that I find myself thankful he isn't a "traditional" Arab and dresses like an "American" instead. I'm sad that traditional Arabs are scared to be seen in public right now. I fear that my baby boy will grow up in this country that I love so much and be hurt by the people in it just because of his name.

I am not writing this for those who are preju-diced—the ignorant generally stay ignorant. I am writing this to those who already know what I'm talking about. I'm writing this to those who under-stand what's important and what makes a person good.

I am pleading with you to not let this continue.

I'm asking you to not turn a blind eye or a deaf ear. If you see or hear something happening, do something to stop it. And that ranges all the way from snide remarks to fire bombs. Don't let them spread their hatred around. I love my family and want to be able to speak their names loudly and proudly. Please help me to be able to do that again without fear.

Thanks for listening, and God bless America.

"I was watching the flight path of my wife's plane on the American Airlines Web site, tracking the altitude and speed, when the image disappeared. The screen said, 'Please contact American,' and I just knew."

—BOSTON RESIDENT, *Newsday* 9/13/2001

FROM AN AOL POST, 9/16/2001 4:08 PM
EASTERN DAYLIGHT TIME
SUBJECT: FROM A UNITED STATES MARINE

I am a United States Marine.
  We are supposed to be the toughest group of

people that ever walked the face of the this planet, but I have feelings.

I am hurting like the rest of you.

Can I see another's woe,
And not be in sorrow too?
Can I see another's grief,
And not seek for kind relief?

—WILLIAM BLAKE,
"ON ANOTHER'S SORROW"

FROM AN AOL POST, 9/15/2001 8:17 PM
EASTERN DAYLIGHT TIME
SUBJECT: PLEASE PRAY FOR COLLEEN

Please pray for our niece, Colleen Deloughery, murdered in WTC tower 2. Please pray for her two small children, who wait at the window for her to come home at night, and cry for their mommy. Please pray for her husband, who doesn't know how to comfort his children, while he cries for his wife.

Please pray for her mother-in-law, who shouldn't have to bury a daughter, and who cries for her son and grandchildren at night.

Please pray for her brothers and sister, who have had a lifetime of sorrow, and never expected to lose another family member.

Please pray that Colleen didn't suffer, and that her final thoughts were of her family.

Please pray for the rest of us left behind, that we can find comfort in the fact that Colleen is in a far better place now, and that she is always with us.

＊

FROM AN AOL POST, 9/16/2001 1:15 PM
EASTERN DAYLIGHT TIME
SUBJECT: BECAUSE OF YOUR STRENGTH,
        WE ARE FINDING OURS

Everyone has been through a gamut of thought and emotion during this past week. The topics of conversation were unfamiliar and "unreal."

To find a light out of this darkness has been more than a small challenge, but there was something that helped us to find that—the people who took action on flight 93. Their efforts were not only important in a physical way—they allowed the American people to feel strength at a time when the strongest of us were struggling to feel that.

I am glad to find a place where I can write these words and my whole family can express the overwhelming gratitude we feel. Since there are no words to fully communicate our feelings to these people and their families, we must settle for Thank You . . . so very much . . . you are in our thoughts . . . you are remembered.

✳

FROM AN AOL POST, 9/15/2001 1:05 AM
EASTERN DAYLIGHT TIME
SUBJECT: TO DANIEL

D^{an,}
    Wherever you have gone, please wait for me there. Tonight I swear it feels as if I am not long behind you. I love you.

✳

"Everyone either knows someone or knows someone who knows someone who was in the World Trade Center. It's made the world a very small place."

—WITNESS TO THE COLLAPSE, 9/11/2001

FROM AN AOL POST, 9/15/2001 1:10 AM
EASTERN DAYLIGHT TIME
SUBJECT: BEST FRIEND LOST

I lost my closest and most dearest friend. His name was Michael, and he was visiting his mother at the WTC on September 11, 2001, when the first plane hit.

I tried calling his mother that day, but could not get through. When I finally got through, all I got was her voice mail.

On September 12, 2001, his mother called me to tell me that Michael had passed away. I tried to control my emotions, but it was very hard, I blew up at work to co-workers who were being very insensitive. His mother told me that he saved her life by pushing her out of the first-floor door, when suddenly the walls caved in and Michael was left under them. Because of the extensive internal bleeding, the doctors were unable to help. He died 13 hours later.

My only regret is that I never got to say good-bye to my friend.

Michael, I know that you are watching me. I just want you to know that I Love You and Will Miss You always.

FROM AN AOL POST, 9/15/2001 12:51 AM
EASTERN DAYLIGHT TIME
SUBJECT: IN MEMORY OF STEVEN D. "JAKE"
JACOBY, COO METROCALL

Just a few hours ago today I read that a friend/former client, Steven D. ("Jake") Jacoby, was on the flight that left Dulles Airport and crashed into the Pentagon. He was the COO of Metrocall.

When I worked as an attorney in Washington, D.C., Jake was my client. I was lucky enough to have worked with him almost daily over a two-year period, preparing financing documents, visiting with lenders and venture capitalists, attending board meetings, and speaking frequently throughout the day by phone on business issues. He and his colleagues went on to create one of the largest paging companies in the country.

During that time, Jake was a true friend. In conservative Washington, D.C., others didn't know what to say about my decision to go through with a "single-parent" pregnancy. But he was kind enough and true enough to his faith to encourage me through a lonely pregnancy; I remember how touched I was that Jake made sure to send me flowers on the day my child was born.

When I returned to my home state six months after my daughter was born, Jake continued to send work my way because he was loyal and knew that I needed to support my child. He was a compassionate gentleman who understood the value of life and the dreams of most Americans.

Jake is survived by his wife and their three young children. Please pray for them.

❋

FROM AN AOL POST, 9/14/2001 11:00 AM
EASTERN DAYLIGHT TIME
SUBJECT: KARLETON D. B. FYFE

I've known Karleton since he was about 10 years old. The day after the attack on the WTC towers, I found myself standing in the doorway to my pantry. At my age, this often happens, and I tried to remember what it was I going into the pantry for.

Then I realized that on some deeper level a higher power was directing my attention to the pantry doorjamb. Many of the Fyfe children had stood dutifully against the doorjamb over the years as they were measured, their height, the date, and their initials recorded there in pencil. Karleton's first measurement, I saw, was dated 1975. He was barely four feet tall. By 1987—his initials and the date in my own handwriting—he was three inches taller than I am.

The shock of discovering that Karleton had perished in the terrorist attack was unlike anything I've ever felt. How could this happen? Even my sister and friends, people who'd barely known Karleton, felt the loss profoundly, telling me that it had made personal an otherwise incomprehensible event.

In all the years I knew Karleton, he was unfailingly cheerful and positive in his outlook, and he never seemed to outgrow his rather mischievous and childlike sense of humor. I have no doubt but that he'll be greatly missed.

Just a day or so before he left us, he and his wife posted new photos of their toddler online. And then he was suddenly gone. I don't know that I'll ever come to terms with the senselessness of it.

To the Fyfes, to the Hamiltons, and to all those touched by the loss of Karleton, my sincerest, my most profound condolences. All of us who knew him understand that a generous and loving and very original spirit was taken from us on Tuesday. Speaking for myself, it's so difficult to grasp, to understand that Karleton is gone. I know that I'll never forget him. Ever.

❋

"We were two blocks from the collapse, and the dust and debris were flying toward us. I could barely see as I was running, then suddenly a building super was opening a door for us and we dove inside. I don't know who he was, but he saved us."

—A FIREFIGHTER FROM BROOKLYN,
New York Magazine 9/24/2001

❋

I propose that each of us commit to doing one random act of kindness each day in honor of someone who died on September 11.

If we all do this, and if we do it for all 7,000 people, that will be almost 18 years of kindness from each one of us. It's a totally simple way to change the world, and it would give some purpose to the senseless deaths we all witnessed.

HEROIC

"We have never been braver. We've never been stronger."

—Mayor Rudolph W. Giuliani,
The New York Times 9/18/2001

FROM AN AOL POST, 9/16/2001 8:35 PM
EASTERN DAYLIGHT TIME
SUBJECT: WHAT HAPPENED IN THE FINAL
           MOMENTS TO YOUR LOVED
           ONES

What Happened September 11, 2001
    To those of you who lost loved ones in the
attack on the World Trade Center and the Pentagon,

here's what happened in their final moments.

Your father was a hero. When the building shook from the blast, he did not concern himself with fear. He helped unblock an office door which had been barricaded by debris and furniture that had moved. He freed three people.

Your friend who was on the plane being hijacked recognized immediately how serious the matter was and reached to calm the shaking hand of the person in the next seat.

Your wife saw a man bleeding from his head, and she tore a piece from her shirt and made a bandage for him.

Your aunt helped her co-workers who could not find the exit through the smoke—they all made it. Then she went back for others.

Your nephew who was the pilot on the plane had only the safety of everyone on board in focus every second.

Your grandfather found a young man pinned under a fallen piece of ceiling, and even when the young man said to go on without him, he stayed until others heard the calls and came to help.

Your husband took on the hijackers, believing that it would cost him his life. He helped save hundreds of people that none of you will ever know.

Your grandmother who worked at the Pentagon led hundreds who were physically stronger to a secure area, putting them before her own welfare, as she always has.

Your uncle gave his water to a choking woman, who gave him God's blessing with every floor they arrived at, arm in arm.

Your brother who always wanted to be a policeman knew without doubt as he followed the cries for help up the stairs that this was the moment why.

Your sister searched her entire floor to make sure everyone was out of there before she began to make her own way down.

Your friend held the exit door open for his office mates with his wheelchair, cheering as they moved on that "We'll all get out together." And he didn't so much hold on to those who lifted him down as hug them.

Your son would not let the tired woman stop. He cajoled, telling her that she reminded him of you and how you two had to meet. He even called her "Mom" to keep her moving.

Your flight attendant daughter was forced to the back of the plane with all the others on board but stood in front of them in protective defiance, keeping herself between the terrorists and her passengers.

Your sister climbed back up three flights against the crowd and the heat, in the belief that her assistant was still there.

Your college buddy's sense of humor kept all in his voice's range smiling and moving with hope.

Your niece provided a shoulder to lean to a man she had seen in the elevator so many times but whose name she never knew.

Your sister-in-law saw a man sitting in the stairwell coughing, and shared her asthma medicine. They moved on together.

Your firefighter brother-in-law helped hundreds of people out, redirecting them to clearer exits as he climbed higher and higher.

Your nephew and his boss carried an older woman 38 floors.

Your cousin got everyone to sing "The Long and Winding Road" as they worked their way down, making up the words they didn't know.

Your mother's last thoughts were the same thoughts she had as she lay her head down every night since you were born.

You wonder what happened. You want to know

what these people you love were feeling, what they were thinking, what they went through in their final moments.

These are actual facts, exactly has they happened. As true as their love for you. As true as their faith in your love for them.

> *"I was in a wheelchair, on the 46th floor. Two of my coworkers carried me down, through all the heat in the stairwell. I kept telling them to go on ahead, but they wouldn't leave me behind."*
>
> —SURVIVOR FROM TOWER 2, 9/12/2001

FROM AN AOL POST, 9/15/2001 4:15 AM
EASTERN DAYLIGHT TIME
SUBJECT: WE ARE ALL HEROES

Wednesday night, as nine other EMTs and paramedics and I were being driven home from the World Trade Center disaster, not much was said among us. Many of us had been there almost 20 hours, but still we did not want to leave.

The pain that I feel is unbearable. I feel that there is more that I should have done. I am sure that this sentiment was shared by my co-workers.

As we drove up the West Side, I was so touched by the people who were in the streets holding signs of love and appreciation for us. They screamed to me that New York loves us and that we are heroes. Being a native New Yorker, I was not accustomed to that kind of outpouring of love and genuine affection. I am a little warmer inside knowing that all of my wonderful country is praying for me, my fellow rescuers, and, of course, the innocents who were so wrongfully taken from us.

I cannot cry any more, and I am sure that I will never be the person I was. But let me say this to all of you who read this: I love you all too and pray for all of us. Without your prayers, I cannot go on. We are all heroes, not just the ones at the WTC, but all the people who make up this great nation of ours.

"I was thinking we were doomed because there were so many people on the stairs and it wasn't moving. Dozens and dozens of firefighters were running past us, telling us to stay calm and keep moving. I remember looking into their eyes, thinking how brave they were."

—A WORKER FROM THE 83RD FLOOR OF THE
WORLD TRADE CENTER TOWER 2,
New York Magazine 9/24/2001

✳

FROM AN AOL POST, 9/14/2001 1:40 AM
EASTERN DAYLIGHT TIME
SUBJECT: I WAS THERE!

I am a chief officer in the New York City Fire Department. I arrived at the scene at approx. 9:10 AM, minutes after the second plane struck Tower 2.

We were setting up a command post on West Street, just opposite the South Tower. Units dispatched from Brooklyn started to arrive and were being deployed to begin to enter the South Tower. Another chief who was with me decided to lead the newly arrived Brooklyn units into the building. I remained at the command post to coordinate the arrival of additional units dispatched to the scene.

I remember thinking, "How do you attack 30 floors of fire 70 stories above street level?"

Suddenly there was a loud noise, and I looked up to see the whole building splitting apart. It seemed that everything was going in slow motion. Tons of glass, steel and concrete falling from the sky directly above us. I turned to run, knowing all along that there was no way I could outrun a 110 story-building coming to the ground.

All I can remember was being knocked to the ground, with pieces of debris landing all around me, until the whole world went black in a choking dust cloud. I remember a firefighter yelling out "I don't want to die here" and me responding "Neither do I, brother." Well, we didn't. All I can say is that I'm still here by the grace of God—I wish I could say the same for the other chief and the firefighters who entered the building only seconds before me.

Officially they are listed as "missing." I ask anyone who reads this post to pray for their souls and for their loved ones to help them accept that these men died doing the work that they loved. "Greater love hath no man than to lay down his life for his neighbor."

I am proud to have known such heroes.

"I will never look at a firefighter the same way again. What is it in someone, hundreds of them, to compel them to run into a burning building while everyone else is running out, just to save people they don't even know? Their bravery has become part of our collective national legacy. Their bravery dignifies us all."

—THE REVEREND BILL HYBELS,
WILLOW CREEK COMMUNITY CHURCH,
SOUTH BARRINGTON, ILLINOIS,
The New York Times 9/17/2001

FROM AN AOL POST, 9/17/2001 10:35 AM
EASTERN DAYLIGHT TIME
SUBJECT: TO THE FAMILY OF FDNY CHIEF
GANSI: THANK YOU

My husband, a fireman from Brooklyn, was in the first collapse. He survived.

As he was climbing out to safety, Chief Gansi was in front of the building. He waved to my husband and gave orders which led him in a different direction from where he was headed—and as a result of those orders, his life was saved.

Our deepest sympathy and gratitude. I am forever grateful.

✳

FROM AN AOL POST, 9/23/2001 1:57 PM
EASTERN DAYLIGHT TIME
SUBJECT: MY FATHER, MY HERO

My dad was a NYC fire captain. On September 11, he rushed into the WTC to try to help rescue others. He never made it out.

Out of the 12 men from his company who went into the building, only 2 of their bodies were found, including my dad's. I guess we are pretty lucky in that respect. I'd just like to say thanks to all the people helping my family get through this and to all the people doing anything to help during this time of crisis and mourning.

✳

"*But in a larger sense, we cannot dedicate, we cannot consecrate, we cannot hallow this ground. The brave men, living and dead, who struggled here, have consecrated it far above our poor power to add or detract.*"

—ABRAHAM LINCOLN, GETTYSBURG
ADDRESS

FROM AN AOL POST, 9/20/2001 3:02 PM
EASTERN DAYLIGHT TIME
SUBJECT: BROTHERS: A POEM WRITTEN
BY A FIREFIGHTER

They were my brothers, I knew not their
names.
They took a job they loved, not for for-
tune or fame.

Respond to the Trade Center without
hesitation,
Bear witness to a scene of utter devastation.

Stretch lines to the upper floors and it
will be hot,
Not knowing yet this was an evil man's plot.

Then out of nowhere, a second plane in,
Sealing the fate of those still within.

And in an instant, the buildings they fell,
In a cloud of smoke and fire reminiscent
of hell.

We will pray for the families of those
who were lost,
Freedom and liberty at such a high cost.

They had a job, they went to work,
heroes all the same,
for they were my brothers, I knew not
their names.

*

*"Firefighters are the first lines of defense. They do
the things that you and I would never do. They run
up in the World Trade Center after a jumbo jet
flies into it. They're running up as people are flee-
ing. What more can be said?"*

—PETE JANHUMEN, INTERNATIONAL ASSO-
CIATION OF FIRE FIGHTERS SPOKESMAN,
Salon.com 9/13/2001

FROM AN AOL POST, 9/17/2001 7:34 PM
EASTERN DAYLIGHT TIME
SUBJECT: THANK YOU TO OUR HERO

My wife and I would like to thank the police officer or fireman who picked up our daughter who had fallen and kept her moving away from the first tower as it came down.

You may have saved her life.

I know you saved ours.

You are our hero, whoever you are.

FROM AN AOL POST, 9/17/2001 7:21 PM
EASTERN DAYLIGHT TIME
SUBJECT: FALLEN HEROES

This is to all of the NY Finest and the NY Bravest. One of whom is my dad.

To My Dad, My Hero

You give it all, although there is so much to bear.

You search beneath the rubble and the sights you encounter, others wouldn't dare.

You are a picture of strength to all, not just to me.

But when you look in the mirror, I know that is not what you see.

I've wondered where you are these past few nights. Especially in the wind and the cold,

Yet even through the chill and darkness, I know you'll never fold.

I think about how wonderful it is to have a Dad as compassionate as you,

One who goes the distance, always, through and through.

I know it is selfish of me, you see

I wish you were home with Mom and me.

Be strong; hold your head up,

Know when you come home, our flag will be flying high.

For those who have lost their lives,

And for those who were ready and willing to die.

*

"Before the collapse, I remember a police offer jumping on top of me. He saved my life, and I never saw him again."

—AN OFFICE WORKER FROM THE 80TH FLOOR
WHO HAD ALMOST MADE IT TO THE BOTTOM OF
ONE WORLD TRADE CENTER, *Newsday* 9/13/2001

As an active duty Army pilot, I am inspired by the heroism of all the brave men and women on the planes, in the buildings, and in the rescue efforts since this terrible event took place on September 11, 2001.

For twelve years of service, I have asked myself what circumstances would allow me to face death without even a second of hesitation while carrying out my mission. The passengers of the downed aircraft in Pennsylvania recognized their fate and took action. I only hope when death greets me, that I will face it with such dignity and bravery.

This demonstration of courage has given me a reason to continue to serve my country. I have never been so proud of my country or my fellow citizens.

FROM AN AOL POST, 9/15/2001 12:54 AM
EASTERN DAYLIGHT TIME
SUBJECT: THE MANY UNSUNG HEROES

I am writing this as I have just returned from the World Trade Center site, spending the last four days searching the rubble in the hopes of finding some sign of life, of hope, of ANYTHING. I am a firefighter and emergency medical technician, and even though I am ONLY a volunteer, I believe that helping others is my moral and civic duty.

However, while searching through the rubble, I realized that America has its values a little backwards. We pay millions of dollars to athletes just because they have that "special skill" of running after a ball, or hitting one. While they earn the millions, we—professional firefighters and EMS personnel—make barely enough to live off, but you won't hear us complain.

I think that EMS personnel should make a little more than they currently do because, day in and day out, we respond to emergencies, never knowing just what to expect, and not worrying about it, because it's our job. We go to situations that most people are running from, while we are running directly into it, "just because we want to help."

FROM AN AOL POST, 9/21/2001 10:16 AM
EASTERN DAYLIGHT TIME
SUBJECT: TRIBUTE TO NYC: YOU
            ANSWERED YOUR LAST CALL

(Dedicated to the brave NYC firefighters who gave
their lives in the line of duty September 11, 2001 at
the World Trade disaster)

I remember the alarm on that fateful day,
As we responded in haste, to be carried away.
With sirens screaming our advancing pace,
We answered the call by taking our place.
We have answered this call many times
    before,
You see it's our job, we expect no less, no
    more.
We know the danger that comes with the
    quest,
But we answered that call, by doing our best.
We are armed with the weapons of life-saving
    gear,
The voices of so many, calling us near.
Then we arrived at this god-awful sight,
The towers ablaze, no time for fear, just
    fight.

This was an act of evil, so many souls could
   be lost,
We must strive to save as many, at whatever
   the cost.
Into the lobby, and then down the hall,
I rush up the steps, to answer the call.
My heart is now pounding, the sweat pours
   down my face,
But I keep moving at a life-saving pace.
Shouting out orders as I continue my quest,
"GET DOWN, KEEP MOVING!" I shout,
"PLEASE GOD! HELP ME!" I'm doing my best.

Then all at once I hear a thunderous roar
   from above,
My life flashes before me, images of those
   whom I love.
Then out of nowhere I am led by the hand,
by this unknown person, who is this man?
He carried me out of this inferno from hell,
As he lifted my soul, just when everything
   fell.
Now I am at peace, just comfort, no pain,
Who is this man who offered his hand when
   my tears fell like rain?

I now stand before this bright heavenly light,
To raise my head and ask, who came to my
   plight?
Then I hear a voice speak from above as my
   eyes roam,
"My Son, do not fear, for he has taken you
   home.

"He's just like you, you see.
He answered my call.
He was just doing his job, giving his all.
His boots and his helmet were supplied from
   above,
And his power and strength came from
   those that you love.
You see, even up here when the alarm bell
   rings,
They answer your call, these firefighters with
   wings.
He carried you away from that horrible
   place,
when you cried out to ME, for my love and
   my grace.

"Your mission is over, my Son,
You answered your last call.

You saved so many lives, walk tall and be
    proud.
My Son, take my hand and walk into the
    light,
And dwell with me forever in GOD'S heav-
    enly might."

*

"The truly fearless think of themselves as normal."

—MARGARET ATWOOD,
"THE WHIRLPOOL RAPIDS"

*

FROM AN AOL POST, 9/15/2001 8:12 PM
EASTERN DAYLIGHT TIME
SUBJECT: RE: FATHER MYCHAL JUDGE

I cannot tell you what a loss for you that you
didn't have the pleasure of knowing or meeting
Father Judge. Unfortunately, my interaction with
him was under awful circumstances.

He was friends with my father, who endured
two terrible illnesses, the second resulting in his
death. During both times of illness, Father Judge

came to visit with my dad in the hospital. My father was a wonderful singer, with a great love of music, and Father would come to sing to him, to lift his spirits, to let my dad know that he was loved.

The very first time I met Father Judge was outside an elevator in the hospital. He had never seen me before, and upon learning my identity, he immediately placed his big hand on my head and prayed for me, my father, and my family. He then gave my mother and me gold Celtic crosses to pin to our lapels. I still have them.

Throughout the entire time Dad was sick, he was there for Dad. And us. Dad and he visited. He would call to see how Dad was doing, and later, after his death, to see how my mom was doing.

And when my father (a retired fire marshal for the City of New York and member of the FDNY Emerald Society Pipes and Drums) passed away, I called Father Judge and told him we would love it if he would deliver the mass. He told me he would be honored.

Father Judge delivered an incredibly beautiful eulogy about the most important man in my life, and it was personal. It was filled with stories of who my dad was and what he meant to Father Judge and all of us. And it was sincere.

I know that my story is not unusual. It is one of

many. He was a fine example of what a human being should be, and New York, along with the rest of the world, has suffered a major loss.

*

"We were there about 14 hours straight, battling smoke in the dark. But the most frustrating thing was we had to keep dropping our gear and running for our lives when we wanted to stay and save other lives."

—ANDREA KAISER, A FIREFIGHTER AT THE
PENTAGON, *The New York Times* 9/14/2001

*

FROM AN AOL POST, 9/24/2001 6:04 PM
EASTERN DAYLIGHT TIME
SUBJECT: HEROES ARE EVERYWHERE

I consider my son a hero. What makes him and a lot of his friends heroes is that in just a couple of days they organized an event that took place on Sunday the 16th—a battle of the bands–type of get-together—and made $33,000 for the victims!

There are people all across the country doing things like this, and they are all heroes—they are at the very foundation of what makes this such a great country.

FROM AN AOL POST, 9/23/2001 11:37 PM
EASTERN DAYLIGHT TIME
SUBJECT: WHAT ABOUT THE IRON
WORKERS

My husband is a NY firefighter. His firehouse made a sign:
NYPD FDNY
IRON WORKERS
WILL OF STEEL UNITE TOGETHER.
It's hanging on the American Express Building.
Any firefighter you talk to will tell you: If it wasn't for the steel workers, no bodies would be found . . .

* * *

"People came out and made signs and are cheering the rescue workers on. Every time a vehicle passes—fire, police, even Con Ed—people yell out, 'You are our heroes.'"

—MAN ON THE WEST SIDE HIGHWAY,
Salon.com 9/13/2001

There were many heroes that day. The firemen, police, and EMTs are rightly heralded for their acts of bravery.

But there were thousands of other heroes in the streets of NYC on Sept. 11.

The fact that so many lived is a testimony of the strength and courage of New Yorkers. There was not one lick of mob mentality on the streets. I was there, under WTC 5. Everyone was upset, nervous, but we moved in an orderly fashion without direction. No one trampled another or said "me first."

My brother helped two older co-workers to escape the carnage. He could have made a much speedier escape if he had left them behind, but as he says, that was not an option.

Our mayor, Rudy Giuliani, is the personification of the spirit of NYC. The country heralds his actions, but I saw thousands of ordinary New Yorkers act in heroic fashion as we ran for our lives through the streets of the city we love.

"I was on crutches, and I couldn't get down the stairs. A co-worker I barely knew carried me all the way down to the EMT guys outside."

—A WOMAN WHO WORKED ON THE 64TH
FLOOR OF TOWER 2, *The New York Times*
9/12/2001

FROM AN AOL POST, 9/18/2001 2:37 AM
EASTERN DAYLIGHT TIME
SUBJECT: THEY KNEW THEY WERE GOING
TO DIE

Risking their lives for others was something they had already come to grips with . . . these firefighters bravely climbed farther and farther away from the line of safety. Many knew they were going to die if they stayed—but they did stay.

These are true heroes to the city that employed them; to the department that trained them; to the men who fathered them; to the women who mothered them; to the wives who were a part of them; to the children who loved them.

To the ones who gave their lives so that others may live—thank you.

The firefighters, police officers or EMS workers who perished on Sept. 11, 2001 were NOT heroes that day.

They became heroes the day they first put on a uniform and decided to dedicate their lives to serving the public.

Each one knew the risks involved with this line of work and did not assume this calling for glory or recognition, but simply for the sake of knowing that he might be able to help a fellow human being.

It's too bad that it takes a tragedy for these most honorable men and women to be recognized for their heroism, when it is nothing short of heroic for them to arrive at work each day.

I hope that every time you pass a police station, fire department, ambulance, or hospital, you say a silent prayer of thanks to all who work within. Someday, one of these dedicated professionals may risk his life to save yours.

❋

I am a NYC police officer who is lucky enough to have survived two collapses while trying to help others who had difficulty helping themselves. In addition to all of the firefighters, police, and EMS who assisted in the evacuation of 1 WTC, I would also like to pay tribute to all of the others who were heavily involved who put their necks on the line. These include the following:

WTC security officers

Military personnel

FBI personnel

State police

Various other federal and state law enforcement personnel

With special acknowledgment for those ordinary working people who showed enormous tenacity and heroism in assisting their fellow citizens in the midst of an unimaginable horror.

No words could possibly describe what it was like in there that day. It was an honor to have been by your side.

"I know we're all going to die; there's three of us who are going to do something about it."

—Thomas Burnett, on a cell phone to his wife just before his plane went down outside of Pittsburgh, *Newsday* 9/13/2001

FROM AN AOL POST, 9/20/2001 10:10 AM
EASTERN DAYLIGHT TIME
SUBJECT: LET'S ROLL

I don't know the name of the young man who spoke to a telephone operator before he and some other passengers decided to try to overpower the hijackers. But I did see on TV that his wife said that just before they made the move to take over, the phone operator heard him say "Let's roll!" His wife said this was a quote the young father used quite often at home when he wanted to get the family moving.

I think the cry of "Let's roll" should be the battle cry of our war on terrorism, just like "Remember the Alamo" was to the Texans!

FROM AN AOL POST, 9/19/2001 10:19 AM
EASTERN DAYLIGHT TIME
SUBJECT: THANK YOU FOR THE FIRST OF
THIS WAR'S HEROES

Thank you for resisting. Thank you for calling home and calling out so we may know some of what was happening up there in the skies.

Thank you for making us all PROUD. This can't help your families since they are without you, but thank you for showing us all the thoughts we should have. Not to just let them win. But if we are to die, we die on OUR terms, NOT theirs.

***

FROM AN AOL POST, 9/16/2001 3:22 PM
EASTERN DAYLIGHT TIME
SUBJECT: ACCIDENTAL HEROES

I am so impressed and proud of the goodness and bravery of those men (and women) on the plane that crashed in Pennsylvania. Wow! In the span of 30 to 45 minutes, with knowledge of what had happened to the WTC from cell phone conversations, they formed a team and decided to take their chances by acting to disrupt the hijackers, who certainly were headed for the White House or Capitol.

They did it for their country and to save other lives. They did that knowing they were going to die. They acted for what was right, in the face of what must have been their abject terror. The fact that they could act in that way is an example to me of the grace of God and the heroism that lies deeply within all of us.

There was also something peculiarly American to me about that act or maybe it was just the last words of one of those accidental heroes who said something like "Ready guys? Let's roll."

But we'd be kidding ourselves if we didn't acknowledge that the propensity to act for evil is in all of us as well. It's up to us to choose which path we'll take; those choices often present a very slippery slope.

My heart goes out to the families of these heroes. I'm sure you knew of their goodness and bravery. Now the whole country does and unites to thank these extraordinary patriots.

I am a female soldier in the US Army. I have to say—not out of selfishness for myself, but as a member of the greatest military in the world—that I am amazed that we have all pulled together as one during this, civilians and military alike.

However, I believe that civilians are forgetting what lies ahead: a war that will probably involve biological warfare and the loss of many, many lives. The military are about to become the next victims, and heroes, as well.

As a soldier, I am fearful. I think I can speak for most military members when I say that we are all scared. Most of us have been taught to be strong and never show weakness, but in us all is a fear of the unknown. We really have no idea what exactly we are up against.

I myself do not fear dying for something I believe in: the freedom of the United States. But in talking with other soldiers I have realized that as they prepare for war, their mothers, fathers, sisters, brothers, friends, and relatives are grieving for the possible loss of their loved ones in the same way that the victims of the WTC and Pentagon are.

As you all slowly begin to pick up the pieces of your lives, please don't forget that other families are not so lucky. The fear will be in them until this is resolved and our soldiers are brought home. It takes a strong parent to send one's own off to fight a war and risk their lives, and a stronger parent to support the effort their children are giving.

I fear that our guys will be overlooked by the majority of the population, as are the guys in Kosovo and Bosnia. I urge all of you to remember and pray, on a daily basis, for the military and their families until each and every one returns home, be it as a victim or hero—don't let them be forgotten over time. We all need your support and prayers now.

FROM AN AOL POST, 9/15/2001 10:10 PM
EASTERN DAYLIGHT TIME
SUBJECT: RUNNING FOR HIS LIFE BUT
STOPPED TO HELP

This is a short tale of Ed Cooke, an electrician who was on the 52nd floor of the second tower to be hit. The plane slammed into the 80th floor above him. He and his buddy started running to the stairs and down as fast as they could.

Ed stopped to help an older guy who was having difficulty going down the stairs. Ed stayed with him, watching firefighters pass them heading upwards; he got the guy a shot of oxygen and made sure he rested every ten floors or so until he got his breath back.

Both Ed and this man made it out just minutes before the building collapsed. These are unsung heroes, with their deeds going unnoticed, and watched only by God.

*

*"The bravest are the tenderest
The loving are the daring"*

—BAYARD TAYLOR, "SONG OF THE CAMP"

FROM AN AOL POST, 9/15/2001 10:13 PM
EASTERN DAYLIGHT TIME
SUBJECT: LADDER CO. 8, 1ST UNIT AT WTC

They were responding to a reported gas leak, and were testing at a sewer. There was a French cameraman with them, looking for footage of a fire, as he had been all week. Suddenly a jet flew over, very low. They all looked up, as the Frenchman continued to roll tape. Watching in horror and awe, Ladder Co. 8 (from the Tribeca section of New York City) saw the jet fly into the WTC.

This is the real story behind the only video of the first crash.

My nephew—my hero—and his company did not have to wait to be dispatched.

They were in full gear and the rig was running. They were first to arrive at the crash site and immediately went into the building.

I was just waking up and having my coffee when I turned the TV on. (I'm a NYC subway train engineer, and Tuesday was my day off.) I was shocked, and immediately worried about my nephew, who lives in an apartment in my house. He was 25 years old, a volunteer fireman for two years already; he'd only been out of the fire academy for 2 months, following in the footsteps of his deceased father, a decorated firefighter.

I watched as the phone rang. My sister called from Manhattan to make sure that her son wasn't working. I couldn't lie to her. Then WTC 2 went down. I could not believe that after withstanding the impact of the plane, it still went down.

Shortly after that, my sister called again. Thankfully, Jim called her and said, "Mom, I'm okay, I'm on the 30th floor of WTC 1."

Fifteen minutes later, the second WTC building, #1, went down. For an hour and 45 minutes, we waited and watched this nightmare unfold. Then my sister called—she saw Jim on NBC news, and he was ALIVE!

Thursday night he came home for a little while and we talked. They never got the order to get out, but they sensed that it was time to go; the other building, the second one to get hit, had gone down what seemed like a long time ago. He ran down the stairs and reached the exit as the building came down around him. The fireman behind him received burns to the back of his neck. The firefighters behind him did not make it out.

This is the story of my nephew, the NYC hero firefighter.

I am a New Jersey police officer who spent many long hours at "Ground Zero" with a shovel looking for anyone who may have survived. The scene was so horrific that I could only describe it to my wife as a peek at the end of the world. But I believe that there are some real heroes who need to be recognized:

- above all, the innocent men and women who gave their lives to help others when everything was exploding around them
- the firefighters and police officers who gave their lives to save people they never even met
- the civilian volunteers—the iron workers, construction workers, Red Cross volunteers, and all the other people who simply came out to help in any way they could

There was a teenage girl from the Red Cross who was there when I got there and was still there when I was leaving. She was handing out food, coffee, etc., and cleaning up after the exhausted workers who were going back to the rubble. This young lady and her fellow volunteers are true heroes.

They exemplify the spirit of America: the readiness to help others despite the toll it takes on them.

I thank all of those dedicated, caring people who helped keep everyone going in this monumental effort. God bless you all.

*

FROM AN AOL POST, 9/17/2001 8:39 AM
EASTERN DAYLIGHT TIME
SUBJECT: RESCUE DOGS

Please remember that these rescue dogs are our heroes as well. Sadly, one of the Coast Guard's search dogs perished last night due to heat exhaustion. The animals work tirelessly and to the point of exhaustion. One rescuer was interviewed last night on TV. At his side was his exhausted dog, laying on its side, completely worn out. These animals do all this hard work out of their undying love for humans.

They are walking on very hot rubble and steel sharp enough to cut their feet. They do not stop and sit down when they get tired—they keep going as well.

On television they just showed live pictures from the WTC disaster site. Two rescuers were bringing their search dogs into the rubble, and one fireman turned from what he was doing and patted each dog as it went by, to show his appreciation of the hard work they are doing.

Don't forget our four-legged heroes!

FROM AN AOL POST, 9/23/2001 7:42 PM
EASTERN DAYLIGHT TIME
SUBJECT: WHAT THEY REDEFINED . . .

When I used to ask my little sister who her hero was, she'd say (with all the enthusiasm she could muster in her tiny body) "SpongeBob Square Pants"—a child cartoon character.

Across the schools of America you could have walked into any fourth-grade classroom and asked that question. I guarantee you would have heard something along the lines of "Pokemon" or "Powerpuff Girls"—but not today.

These men and woman have redefined the term "hero"; they have placed it back into that special category opposite "saint" and "angel." Their courage and humanity have opened our eyes to what a real hero should be.

When your little sister can look at you and say "Those men are my heroes," then you know something special, something truly amazing has managed to reach in and touch all of America's hearts. Those men and woman who are still digging through the rubble, who haven't slept, who continue to work day in and day out for people they've never met are the true heroes of today.

I want to say thank you and God bless.

＊

FROM AN AOL POST, 9/20/2001 2:29 AM
EASTERN DAYLIGHT TIME
SUBJECT: TRIBUTE

As a firefighter in NYC for 38 years—now retired, but with a son and son-in-law now in the front lines—I think these words of Rudyard Kipling really express the brotherhood that is theirs, and was mine:

"I have eaten your bread and your salt, I have drunk your water and wine,

The deaths you died I have watched beside, and the lives you lived were mine"

In memory and gratitude for the years with

some of the bravest, most compassionate men on earth . . .

FROM AN AOL POST, 9/14/2001 9:37 PM
EASTERN DAYLIGHT TIME
SUBJECT: BEING A HERO'S LITTLE GIRL

Eight years ago I was faced with a tragedy I thought for sure I would never see again. My father, a fireman, was at the first WTC bombing doing what he loved, saving peoples lives. He came home about 20 pounds lighter but in one piece.

On Tuesday morning it started all over. My father—still a fireman—and my brother, an EMT, were some of the first on the scene.

Daddy pulled a woman out of a burning car, turned around to his truck, and the WTC fell on his head. I am a lucky one. He is alive, and will heal.

My father fought in war, saved a man from an explosion some 30 years ago (suffering severe burns), and did countless other heroic things just by being a fireman. My father will take a long time to heal, but he has no plans of retirement.

I am my father's princess, and he will always be my hero—now he is yours, too.

FROM AN AOL POST, 9/14/2001 10:55 PM
EASTERN DAYLIGHT TIME
SUBJECT: RE: BEING A HERO'S LITTLE GIRL

You are so lucky to be blessed with such a father. And he to have such a gracious daughter.

I remember one of my daughter's classmates asking her close friend, "Why would your father want to be a firefighter? What money is there in that?"

I've always wished I could have been there to answer that silly boy.

Being a hero is a greater reward than any money could bring. You get to save a life, maybe many lives.

There is an Indian saying that goes something like, when you save a life, you become responsible for that life, or something to that effect. This is joy, this is bliss. To look in another's eyes and see life, a life you have been instrumental in preserving, must be tantamount to reaching out and touching the face of God.

This service and sacrifice raises us and those around us up to the clouds. Of course, there are those who would argue it is human nature to be selfish. But I have heard it said that nature is what we are put here to rise above. And I truly believe this of your father.

God Bless him and those like him.

"Courage is the ladder on which all the other virtues mount."

—CLARE BOOTH LUCE, *Reader's Digest,* 1979

LOVING

"It is time to hug your neighbor and embrace your nation."

—Bob Hope, *Salon.com* 9/24/2001

FROM AN AOL POST, 9/19/2001 5:17 PM
EASTERN DAYLIGHT TIME
SUBJECT: A NEW AMERICA

In the wake of this tragedy, a renewed spirit of love and patriotism seems to have overtaken us. Even as candles burn in vigil, a more positive spirit seems to be prevailing. Perhaps the younger generation had never before connected with the enduring might of our forefathers from previous eras, who knew what it was to gain strength through adversity.

But now something exciting has awakened. The simple Biblical command to love thy neighbor is an ideal slightly more within reach. The lyrics of the Louis Armstrong classic "Wonderful World"—about friends shaking hands, implicitly saying "I love you"—ring as shafts of light from heaven amidst the smoke and rubble.

We used to wave flags because it was tradition on the 4th of July, and kids used to say the Pledge of Allegiance, holding their hands over their hearts, because the teacher told them to. But they'd become rituals. We'd grow slightly impatient singing the national anthem before baseball and football games, never paying attention to the words "gave proof through the night that our flag was still there." But now we will. And we'll be more patient. Now the song and the image of the waving flag have taken on new meaning.

In my own Los Angeles neighborhood on the Friday night after the terror, hundreds of people lined the boulevard in an impromptu parade of honking, flag waving and shouts of "God Bless America!" America loves a party, but this was no casual Independence Day barbecue. Candles burned along the sidewalk, reminding us what happened, but the palpable determination of hope it awakened led to a swell of joy and the feeling we would somehow all be okay—even if the standards of what defines that have changed.

The terrorists try to change our way of life, to bring out our greatest fears, but as we see, their acts have only made us stronger. If I ever doubted the goodness and potential for selflessness of most people in America and throughout the world, the response to all this—be it prayer, blood, cash and food donations, literal life sacrificed in the civil service duty of rescue, those few brave souls on the plane in Pennsylvania—shows me, beautifully, that love conquers, compassion endures, and heroes still exist. As the Apostle Paul wrote in 1 Corinthians, "love never fails."

*

> *"I am just struck with this city's desire to congregate, to heal. I've never been so proud to be a part of this culture."*
>
> —A MAN WHO HAD JUST BEEN HUGGED BY
> A STRANGER WEARING ANGEL WINGS,
> *The New York Times* 9/14/2001

As we move forward, pray we refrain from mean insults, comments, and violent or angry attacks on people (especially children!) in the U.S. who "look like terrorists" based on their nationality or physical characteristics.

If we attack ourselves (we are made up of all ethnic, racial and religious backgrounds), we are giving into and perpetuating terrorism.

The U.S.A. has learned much about racism, hatred, and infringement on human rights: Hitler's actions against the Jews horrified us. Our own history includes enslaving Africans and decades of prejudice against the Irish, Italians, Jewish, Indians, and other groups. U.S. citizens still suffer from past acts of fear, hatred, and anger toward people of different racial and ethnic origins.

Do not hate your neighbor because of what they look like. Many Middle Eastern people came innocently to the U.S. over the years to flee war, escape religious or political persecution, and to have their children and families safe. The attack on the U.S. is not representative of the peoples of the Middle East, which is made up of many countries.

Terrorists thrive on hatred. As Americans, we have learned to accept differences because we believe in freedom. That is what we are fighting for now: FREEDOM!

If we fight ourselves by hurting people who look different, then the real terrorists succeed: They use us as ammunition (like they used our planes, filled with our citizens) against our own country.

"Darkness cannot drive out darkness; only light can do that. Hate cannot drive out hate; only love can do that."

—MARTIN LUTHER KING, JR.,
Strength to Love, 1963

Many will be asking your opinion of these events. Each question is an opportunity for you to contribute to the love that is in the world or to the fear that is in the world. This is the same opportunity that presents itself to you at each moment.

If you hate those who hate, you become like them. You add to the violence and the destructive energy that now fills our world. As you make the decision to see with clarity and compassion, you will see that those who committed these acts of violence were in extreme pain and that they were fueled by the violent parts of ourselves—the parts that judge without mercy, strike in anger, and rejoice in the suffering of others. They were our proxy representatives. If you can look with compassion upon those who have suffered and those who have committed acts of cruelty alike, then you will see that all are suffering. The remedy for suffering is not to inflict more suffering.

This is an opportunity for a massive expression of compassion. It is also an opportunity for a massive expression of revenge. Which world do you intend to live in—a world of revenge or a world of compassion?

*

> *"Now the entire city is out there cheering and clapping and sending letters and just really show-ing their signs of support for the cops. You know what that's doing for them? It's boosting and enhancing the morale, it's making it, as bad as it is, as tragic as it is, so much better."*

—POLICE COMMISSIONER BERNARD KERIK,
The New York Times 9/17/2001

*

FROM AN AOL POST, 9/15/2001 1:15 AM
EASTERN DAYLIGHT TIME
SUBJECT: I FELL IN LOVE

This week I fell in love with every firefighter on the planet. I want nothing more than to marry a firefighter. They are the most amazing people in the world. I also fell deeply in love with America and NYC. Aren't we just a beautiful brave country?

"There's love in the air."

—WOMAN AT A CANDLELIGHT VIGIL,
Entertainment Weekly 9/28/2001

FROM AN AOL POST, 9/23/2001 12:33 PM
EASTERN DAYLIGHT TIME
SUBJECT: THIS GAVE ME CHILLS! BUT IT'S
TRUE!

Every two weeks I keep my six grandchildren, all under seven years of age, for the night. Last night was the night. As they were all outside talking about what happened—and yes, they all know something bad did—they wanted to know what they could do for the children who died.

I was dumbfounded, and didn't have an answer, so I asked them what they thought they could do. We live in the country, so they looked around for a while, then my six-year-old baby said, "I know, let's pick them some flowers."

So off the six of them went, picking wildflowers until they all had bunches. I asked them what they were going to do with the flowers. They said they were going to send them to the children who died.

I asked them how. And they told me they were going to lay them on the picnic table and have angels pick them up and take them to the children.

I was busying myself trying to get the bonfire ready and make supper, but in the back of my mind, I reminded myself to remove the flowers—even though I felt guilty trying to fool them, I didn't want to break their hearts.

But after the chore of getting six children ready for bed, I forgot about the flowers.

My heart fell to my toes when I heard my granddaughter say this Sunday morning, "Hey guys, I heard a lot of birds' wings last night, lets go see if the angels came and got our flowers."

She opened up the door, and they all started yelling "They're gone! They're gone, Grammy!"

I rejoiced with them, and silently vowed to thank my husband for remembering to remove them. But when I did, he was just as shocked, for he had not done it either.

I do not go to church, but I believe in God and teach the children about God. Did angels take them? I don't know, I just know they were gone. The innocence of a child . . . You decide where they went . . .

"America is a willingness of the heart."

—F. Scott Fitzgerald, *The Crack-up*

FROM AN AOL POST, 9/21/2001 3:17 PM
EASTERN DAYLIGHT TIME
SUBJECT: FROM A 21-YEAR-OLD PAKISTANI
MUSLIM WHO WORKED IN THE
WTC

I was on my back, facing this massive cloud that was approaching. It must have been 600 feet off, and everything was already dark.

I normally wear a pendant around my neck, inscribed with an Arabic prayer for safety; it looks similar to the cross. A Hasidic Jewish man came up to me and held the pendant in his hand and looked at it. He read the Arabic out loud for a second.

What he said next, I will never forget. With a deep Brooklyn accent, he said, "Brother, if you don't mind, there is a cloud of glass coming at us, grab my hand, let's get the hell out of here."

He helped me stand up, and we ran for what seemed like forever without looking back. He was the last person I would ever have thought would help me. If it weren't for him, I probably would have been engulfed in shattered glass and debris.

As the world continues to reel from this tragedy, people in the streets are lashing out.

Not far from my home, a Pakistani woman was run over on purpose as she was crossing the parking lot to put groceries in her car. Her only fault? That she had her head covered and was wearing the traditional clothing of my homeland. I am afraid for my family's well-being within our community. My older sister is too scared to take the subway into work now. My eight-year-old sister's school is under lockdown and armed watch by police.

Violence only begets violence, and by lashing out at each other in fear and hatred, we will become no better than the faceless cowards who committed this atrocity. If it weren't for that man who helped me get up, I would most likely be in the hospital right now, if not dead. Help came from the least expected place, and goes only to show that we are all in this together—regardless of race, religion, or ethnicity.

Ask yourselves now how you can help those people in New York and Washington. You can donate blood, you can send clothing, food, and money. Funds have been set up in the New York area to help the families of fallen firefighters, policemen, and emergency personnel.

The one thing that won't help is if we fight among ourselves, because it is then that we are doing exactly what they want us to do, and I know that nobody here wants to do that.

***

FROM AN AOL POST, 9/15/2001 8:27 PM
EASTERN DAYLIGHT TIME
SUBJECT: HELP HEAL OTHERS

In this time of great confusion and unbelievable emotion, let's remember to lend our hearts to loved ones and neighbors. Let's open up a piece of ourselves and share our love with whoever will take it and particularly to those who won't.

Live.

Breathe.

Love.

Believe.

***

"Love is the vital essence that pervades and permeates, from the center to the circumference, the graduating circles of all thought and action. . . . Love is the talisman of human weal and woe—the open sesame to every soul."

—ELIZABETH CADY STANTON, 1860

*

"There have been people on Fifth Avenue hugging us."

—NEW YORK CITY POLICE OFFICER STEVE
PETRILLO OF THE 19TH PRECINCT,
New York Observer 9/24/2001

*

FROM AN AOL POST, 9/20/2001 9:38 PM
EASTERN DAYLIGHT TIME
SUBJECT: PLEASE GIVE ME YOUR
   THOUGHTS

The Power of One
One
person killed thousands,
made towers fall,

buildings burn,
created fear in our hearts,
and saddened all.

One
flag unites us,
under stars forever shining,
red stripes for the blood shed
forever blazing
white stripes for
the light of hope
in our hearts.

One
person can
end the hate,
love all,
stop the cycle of
killing,
unite us,
and make tomorrow a
better day for all.

One person can do anything. Do what
    you can to help us all.

FROM AN AOL POST, 9/15/2001 4:39 PM
EASTERN DAYLIGHT TIME
SUBJECT: VOICES FROM HEAVEN

Tuesday's news has brought a number of deep emotions out in all of us. I find myself struggling between bouts of anger, confusion, fear, and, of course, sadness. The times when my emotions are the strongest are when I see pictures and hear stories of the victims, and I wonder what they must have gone through on the morning of Tuesday the 11th. But I also wonder what they may be saying now.

If I were to guess, I would say it would be, "Don't let hatred breed more hatred, use my death to create life, use this negativity to create foundations of love and compassion for your fellow man. Use your confusion to create peace."

*

"From the devastated buildings and the crashing airplanes, people cried the most important words they could find. They're the words of love. Love can't fail. Love always wins.

"Today is a day of sorrow, but today is also the day of the victory of love. These people who died by

the terrorist attack aren't victims, they're heroes. They're heroes of love and true humanity. We want them to hear us: We love you, too!"

—The Reverend Vladimir Alexeev, Holy Trinity Orthodox Church, Brooklyn, New York, *The New York Times* 9/17/2001

⁕

FROM AN AOL POST, 9/20/2001 2:21 PM EASTERN DAYLIGHT TIME
SUBJECT: SEEN, BUT NOT THOUGHT OF, MEDIA

When you found out the World Trade Center was attacked, I bet every one of you turned on a TV, turned on a radio, signed online, or some combination thereof.

You turned to the people who are always there in a time of crisis, disaster, celebration—the news reporters. We depend on them to report the news objectively. To not declare anyone wrong or right. To not show emotion.

David Letterman had Dan Rather on his show earlier this week. Dan Rather broke down twice on air. Dan Rather! You just don't expect that.

David Letterman said something to him that brought tears to my eyes and made my heart surge with pride for our news reporters. David said something to this effect, "I know people depend on you to be strong, but, damn it, you're human too."

I want to thank them for this. For being strong. For not letting their voice crack when they report that someone they knew is dead. For staying there at Ground Zero when anyone else in their position would have wanted to run home and hug everyone they could and maybe even cry. For reporting the news that every one of us was riveted to.

*

"I never loved you more, New York!"

—A CARD AMONG FLOWERS, FLAGS AND
PHOTOGRAPHS BY A LAMPPOST ON
HOUSTON STREET, *Newsday* 9/17/2001

GENEROUS

"But a certain Samaritan, as he journeyed, came where he was: and when he saw him, he had compassion on him,

"And went to him, and bound up his wounds . . . and took care of him."

—LUKE 10:33-34

❋

FROM AN AOL POST, 9/15/2001 5:17 PM
EASTERN DAYLIGHT TIME
SUBJECT: THANK YOU FOR SAVING
          MY LIFE

I was frozen, and you stopped and cried, "Run, run, run!" When I didn't move, you grabbed my hand and pulled me along. I ran with you. We ducked into doorways and dodged the falling debris. We didn't stop until we got to Murray Street and ran around the corner.

I turned to look back at Church Street and I let go of your hand.

And then you were gone. I don't know your name. I didn't see your face. I couldn't guess at your age. I didn't notice your race. I only know you saved my life.

Thank you, thank you, thank you. God bless you.

✳

FROM AN AOL POST, 9/24/2001 4:21 PM
EASTERN DAYLIGHT TIME
SUBJECT: I OWE MY LIFE TO THE KIND-
NESS OF A STRANGER

A complete stranger saved my life. I work at 130 Liberty Street, on the 25th floor, which is directly across the street from the WTC. I fell down while I was running from the collapsing building.

A massive cloud came rushing toward us. I could not pick myself off the ground because my legs were numb from running down the 25 flights of my building. I was buried with ash and debris from the collapsed tower.

I thought it was the end of the world. It was so black that you could not see your hand in front of your eyes. I thought I was dying because with every breath I took more ash and debris went down my throat and into my eyes and nose. A stranger tripped over me while I was lying in the darkness on the sidewalk. All of a sudden I felt a hand pick me up off the ground and drag me into a building to safety.

I thank Jesus Christ for my life and for that kind and wonderful stranger.

"Good and kind people outnumber all others by thousands to one. Thus, in what I like to call the Great Asymmetry, every spectacular incident of evil will be balanced by 10,000 acts of kindness, too often unnoted and invisible as the 'ordinary' efforts of a vast majority."

—STEPHEN JAY GOULD,
The New York Times 9/26/2001

FROM AN AOL POST, 9/17/2001 5:29 PM
EASTERN DAYLIGHT TIME
SUBJECT: THANKS, NEW YORK

Lisa and her friend Phyllis escaped from the 19th floor of the Trade Center tower by walking down the stairs.

Police and firefighters kept the crowds calm and moving as rapidly as possible out of the danger zones.

A couple of blocks away, a woman proprietor of a local cleaners storefront let them use the telephone to make a call "anywhere . . . no charge" to let loved ones know they were safe.

A driver in a very crowded SUV insisted on giving them a ride when it was obvious that walking was a struggle.

BLESS YOU ALL for jumping in to render aid during a time of unspeakable horror . . . we will never forget . . .

*

"What is thine is mine, and all of mine is thine."

—PLAUTUS

*

FROM AN AOL POST, 9/16/2001 2:57 PM
EASTERN DAYLIGHT TIME
SUBJECT: GIVING MY REBATE BACK

To those three brave men who fought to save so many lives, I have made out a check to President Bush and sent it off to help pay for the capture of all terrorists. This check is the $300 sent to me as a tax refund. I can't think of a better place to spend it.

※

FROM AN AOL POST, 9/14/2001 5:31 PM
EASTERN DAYLIGHT TIME
SUBJECT: REBATES FOR RELIEF

We got our tax rebate check on Monday 9/10. "How should we spend it?" I thought. Seems so selfish to keep it for ourselves now. We didn't budget for this income—it is like a lucky lottery ticket.

There are 50 million taxpayers sharing $40 billion in checks out there.

Maybe a lot of it has been spent, or at least planned for. But do some math. If two million or so taxpayers sent their refunds to charity for the East Coast victims and rescue costs, a billion dollars could be raised in a week!

I know I won't miss our rebate knowing thousands need it RIGHT NOW far more than we do— I hope many more feel the same. Whether you've already spent the money or are yet to get it, consider who needs it now.

"I'm here to do whatever. I can hold hands, listen to stories, sweep the streets, whatever."

—Former World Trade Center worker
volunteering at Red Cross headquarters, *The New York Times* 9/13/2001

FROM AN AOL POST, 9/17/2001 12:29 AM
EASTERN DAYLIGHT TIME
SUBJECT: AS I WENT THROUGH NEW
YORK . . .

As we passed through, American flags were held high and mounted on cars. While looking at New York, all we saw was smoke. We headed into Connecticut and made a pit stop at McDonalds.

As we were leaving, I saw some firefighters and asked them how to get back on Route 95. They told us they were from Nova Scotia, Canada, and they had just come back from New York.

I wanted to hug them and I knew I couldn't do enough. But my friend and I bought dinner for those 20 firefighters—of course they refused, but we insisted.

God bless this awesome country!

"The greatest grace of a gift, perhaps, is that it anticipates and admits of no return."

—HENRY WADSWORTH LONGFELLOW,
LETTER TO MRS. J. T. FIELDS, 2/28/1871

FROM AN AOL POST, 9/23/2001 10:34 AM
EASTERN DAYLIGHT TIME
SUBJECT: LEMONADE STAND

Yesterday I went to a crafts store. In front of the store sat a family with a lemonade stand. On an average day before September 11, 2001, this may have been a bit odd, but acceptable with the Georgia heat. Only on this day this lemonade stand was different. It was manned by about five young children who held signs saying all donations for the cups of lemonade would go to the Red Cross to help the victims and their families.

I was so touched by their innocence and sincere desire to help. This is the future of America, and they make us proud to be a part of this great nation!

✳

"We were running and running everywhere handing out drinks to the men in ambulances and the firemen."

"I feel kind of happy because we're helping the people who need help."

—CHRISTOPHER, 7, AND HIS COUSIN,
AMANDA, 9, *Newsday* 9/13/2001

FROM AN AOL POST, 9/21/2001 2:33 AM
EASTERN DAYLIGHT TIME
SUBJECT: MAKES ME PROUD TO BE AN
AMERICAN

In this cloud of despair that hangs over our country, shining lights seem to be appearing to guide us through. One such story of American kindness that I wanted to share with my community is of two little girls that I babysit. They wanted to help our country, but what and how could little children help? They decided to do what they love best—baking.

They made cupcakes, brownies, and cookies and walked through their neighborhood to see if anyone would buy their baked goods so that they could raise money for the Red Cross. They went door to door to see if everyone's heavy heart could be lightened with some sweet solidarity and a "God Bless You" to those who helped out in any way they could afford. They carried a full-size American flag with them, one that their dad took off the front of their house.

All five days they walked with their mom after she got off work. They didn't put a price on their baked goodies, but asked for a donation to help the people of the New York City terrorist attacks. To their delight they have collected $400, which will all go to the Red Cross.

This makes me so proud to be an American, and to see how in this time of mourning there are little shining lights that give us hope of better things to come.

"Bear one another's burdens."

—GALATIONS 6:2

FROM AN AOL POST, 9/12/2001 1:10 PM
EASTERN DAYLIGHT TIME
SUBJECT: PRAYERS FROM A 6-YEAR-OLD

Yesterday I had to sit my six-year-old down and explain to her the horrible attack that occurred. We cried together as we watched the TV.

Last night as I walked past her bedroom door, I saw her praying the best she knew how—she asked God to take care of the people who are coming to live with him, and to send blessings to the people who lost someone they love.

I can only hope the prayers of a little girl are heard in the hearts of all the families and friends of people who were lost in this tragedy.

*

> *"Even in the darkest of times we have the right to expect some illumination, and that such illumination may come less from theories and concepts than from the uncertain, flickering, and often weak light that some men and women, in their lives and work, will kindle under almost all circumstances and shed over the time-span that was given them on earth."*

—HANNAH ARENDT, *Men in Dark Times*, 1968

*

FROM AN AOL POST, 9/16/2001 11:39 PM
EASTERN DAYLIGHT TIME
SUBJECT: ONE PERSON DOES MAKE A
DIFFERENCE!

A radio station that was planning to do a concert ticket giveaway on September 12 patriotically decided that an auction to raise money for the Red Cross would be best.

First thing that morning a seven-year-old named Dylan called in and gave $50. The Red Cross and the morning hosts thought that was such a kind thing for a young child to do that they helped out by digging out $20 of their own pockets to make his bid in the auction $70.

This started a chain reaction of callers donating to Dylan's bid, which quickly became "The Dylan Fund for Red Cross." By midmorning the station had to direct people to call direct to the local Red Cross center and tell them it was for the Dylan Donation.

There were so many blessed hearts in and around Roanoke, Virginia, that they soon had collected over $50,000 for the Dylan Donation to Red Cross. All day there were businesses calling and challenging other businesses; professional individuals donating thousands and challenging other individuals in the same profession.

That day alone, due to that one little boy, I heard and witnessed more heroic efforts than I have seen in my entire 33 years of life!

❋

"It is one of the most beautiful compensations of life, that no man can sincerely try to help another without helping himself."

—RALPH WALDO EMERSON

FROM AN AOL POST, 9/15/2001 7:32 AM
EASTERN DAYLIGHT TIME
SUBJECT: PAY IT FORWARD

My cousin had a very interesting experience . . . She was a block south from the south tower when the second plane flew over her head and hit the building. She experienced the terror and horror of that morning like thousands of others in lower Manhattan, but was unhurt.

Somehow she got to the Brooklyn side of the Brooklyn Bridge with no way of getting home to Queens. She stopped a motorist and asked where he was going. He said Bensonhurst. Still far from home but close enough, so she took the ride.

He drove her practically all the way home, a good five miles past Bensonhurst. He was willing to drive her to her doorstep, but a bridge they had to cross was closed except to residents. This kind and brave man did this when no one knew what was going on, everyone was afraid, things were chaotic, and everyone just wanted to be safely at home.

When my cousin was getting out of the car, she asked for his address so she could send him something to thank him. He simply said, "Pay it forward."

If you are not familiar with this expression, it means "Don't pay me back, pay it forward, by doing something good for someone else."

"I saw a group of doctors and nurses who drove all the way up from Kentucky to bring us six bins of gloves and medical supplies."

—VOLUNTEER AT ONE OF THE MANY DROP-OFF POINTS IN MANHATTAN, *The New York Times* 9/14/2001

I was in my car heading to work when, right in front of me, the first plane crashed into the North Tower. It took a few seconds for it to register, but then I pulled over and got out of my car. There was a huge billow of gray smoke pouring out of this gaping hole near the top of the building.

I tried calling my office from my cell phone, but my service was dead. I walked around the corner, found a pay phone, and called them. I told them I just saw a plane crash into the WTC and wasn't going to be on our 9:00 AM conference call. (How such a trivial thing was going through my mind, I will never know!)

I hung up and started walking back to my car when I heard a loud explosion. I ran around the corner to see the second tower on fire. Debris was falling everywhere. People were pointing and gasping as they stared in amazement. I grabbed my disposable camera out of my purse (I always carry one for work purposes) and took a few pictures. It still hadn't really registered what was happening. Then I noticed that some of the "debris" was actually people jumping from the North Tower. I started to get nauseous and turned away.

It was then that I saw a woman in a zombie-like state, walking down the street with blood on her face and shirt. I went to her and asked if she was okay. She was sobbing and kept repeating that she needed to get out of there. I volunteered to drive her to the hospital and walked her back to my car. On the way, she told me how she had been sitting right outside, eating breakfast, when the first plane crashed. She had been hit by the falling debris and glass.

This young woman worked in the WTC and is originally from Hong Kong. She kept asking herself why she came to New York. Her injuries were minor, but she needed to have some glass removed from her arms. I dropped her off at St. Vincent's, where medical workers were lining the streets with stretchers. I then drove to the Upper West Side to get as far away from the madness as possible.

I pray for those missing loved ones and pledge to stand strong with the rest of the nation in the face of this tragedy. God Bless America.

"Do all the good you can, by all the means you can, in all the ways you can, in all the places you can, at all the times you can, to all the people you can, as long as ever you can."

—JOHN WESLEY, *Letters, Rule of Conduct*

*

FROM AN AOL POST, 9/16/2001 12:33 AM
EASTERN DAYLIGHT TIME
SUBJECT: CHILDREN REACHING OUT TO
    HELP

My children, ages 17, 12, and 10, came to me and said, "Mom, how can we help? What can we do to help out?"

I told them we could have a lemonade and cookie stand or maybe a car wash and try and raise some money and send it to the Red Cross. They went to their friends and asked to help. We went out on the street corner with flags and signs and determination to help someone in need.

With lots of shouting and waving signs and American flags, we were able to raise $350 in two hours. It is amazing how the community of Fullerton, California, donated from their hearts. Not even knowing who we were, they were willing to give cash donations so freely.

That is what I see happening all over. It is too bad it takes a trauma with such magnitude to unite our people. I am very touched and saddened by what has happened. It is hard to go about your daily activities when we are all being affected one way or another. It is so terrible what these families are going through. If everyone stops and thinks about how they can help . . .

*

> *"Next thing you know we were bombarded with goods. There were women with babies in the car, guys with construction trucks. We trucked 30,000 pounds of gloves, underwear, masks, food, and drinks."*

—A LONG ISLAND MOVING COMPANY
REPRESENTATIVE WHO OFFERED ON
THE RADIO TO BRING SUPPLIES INTO
MANHATTAN, *Newsday* 9/17/2001

*

I have been a volunteer for two days at Ground Zero, bringing supplies to the workers involved in the rescue attempts. Words can't describe the way it really looks there. The news media is not allowed within about five blocks, so those pictures don't show the true Ground Zero. The closest thing to describe it is that it's like the ride Earthquake in Universal Studios.

The reason people are being kept away from the sight is simple. At one point while I was there they had to evacuate because another building they know is unstable was thought to be falling down. There is no reason for more lives to be lost in this tragedy.

At this time no more volunteers or donations (except respirator masks and monetary donations) are needed. As one example, there are currently over 6 million gallons of water. Volunteers and donations will be needed again in the future, so please be ready when the call goes out.

If you feel you must do something now, there are hundreds of people waving flags and saying thank you to the workers as they leave Ground

Zero. After all the devastation and sadness, seeing the thanks and patriotism is a very uplifting feeling. Please join them if you are in the New York area and want to help. They are some of the most unknown helpers at the sight but truly a very big help.

*

"It's just one minor thing that maybe us football guys could do to help."

—JOE PATROVICH, ISLIP FOOTBALL COACH, ON THE SIX CASES OF WATER, 43 CASES OF SPORTS DRINKS, AND 18 COOLERS FILLED WITH ICE AND GATORADE THAT THE SUFFOLK COUNTY FOOTBALL COACHES ASSOCIATION HAD COLLECTED FOR THE RESCUE WORKERS, *Newsday* 9/13/2001

*

FROM AN AOL POST, 9/19/2001 11:11 PM
EASTERN DAYLIGHT TIME
SUBJECT: LEMONADE AND HAIR
        BARRETTES

My granddaughter's babysitter and the children she cares for had a lemonade stand and raised $82. She also made hair barrettes and ribbons in red, white, and blue and raised over $300. She had our local fire department pick the money up to donate to New York. They came in their truck so the little guys could sit in it and learn what our firefighters do for us.

Not only did she raise money so desperately needed, she taught the kids about love and helping those in need.

*

> *"We helped ourselves to everything we could carry out of this commercial equipment store: cases of gloves, masks, crowbars, pails, and respirators, without a thought of paying for it. The shop owner helped us load it and proudly waved as we drive off."*
>
> —Volunteer rescue worker,
> *Salon.com 9/19/2001*

*

FROM AN AOL POST, 9/19/2001 9:18 AM
EASTERN DAYLIGHT TIME
SUBJECT: MCDONALDS—I HAD AN IDEA!

I work at a McDonalds in Pennsylvania. I was up top in the drive-through (where we take the orders and ring them in) and a man came through with an order that was about $7.

When I went to give this man his change, he looked at me and said, "Put the change in your Red Cross fund."

We didn't have one, so I decided to start my own. But the thing is . . . he gave me a twenty-dollar bill! So whoever this mysterious man is, thank you for starting us out with $13, because at the end of the day, we had around $90! And that is only one day!

I also decided to light candles at McDonalds. All the cars came by and waved and honked their horns and beeped, and some people even had a candle lit in their car! Others who were not allowed to light candles were holding flashlights!

✹

Eighth-graders in a small town in New York are doing a fundraiser . . . selling red, white, and blue ribbons for a dollar each. There are less than 100 kids in each grade and in two grades in two days we have made over $500. I think that is a huge accomplishment . . . I am not bragging; I want to share the idea so people can start something in their own communities.

RESILIENT

*"The ultimate measure of a man is not where he stands
in moments of comfort and convenience, but rather
where he stands at times of challenge and controversy."*

—MARTIN LUTHER KING JR.,
Strength to Love

FROM AN AOL POST, 9/17/2001 9:43 AM
EASTERN DAYLIGHT TIME
SUBJECT: LADY LIBERTY . . . A RAISED FIST
OF DEFIANCE

I stand here in New York Harbor . . . the smolder-
ing ruins a backdrop to my world stage. My arm
is raised high . . . the lamp in my grasp a symbol and

beacon of hope to all who came . . . and still come . . . to my shores, seeking refuge and freedom.

Today it is more than that. Today my arm is a raised fist. A show of defiance. You came to my shores thinking you would destroy me . . . break me, humble me. You thought wrong.

You murdered some of my children . . . but you did not kill my soul.

You destroyed my buildings . . . but not my spirit.

You robbed me of my security . . . but you did not steal my will.

I am America. I was born amidst valor, sacrifice, fire and blood. I have survived much . . . and I will survive you. I do not bow to tyrants nor cater to cowards. Like a phoenix from the ashes I will rise from the ruins that you left behind. Bigger . . . better . . . stronger . . . more powerful than I ever have been before.

So still I stand . . . . .battered but not broken . . . .arm raised high.

"Our greatest glory is not in never falling, but in rising every time we fall."

—Confucius

FROM AN AOL POST FROM A 17-YEAR-OLD,
9/13/2001 10:24 PM EASTERN DAYLIGHT TIME
SUBJECT: MY POEM AND MESSAGE FOR
AMERICA

God bless America
We will not crumble
We will not become ashes
We will not be defeated
We will rise like lanterns
We are the land of the free
And the home of the brave
God holds our quivering country
In the calmness of his arms

"You have to go and participate in the good things."

—Mayor Rudolph W. Giuliani,
9/17/2001

An open letter to a terrorist:
Well, you hit the World Trade Center, but you missed America. You hit the Pentagon, but you missed America. You used helpless American bodies to take out other American bodies, but like a poor marksman, you STILL missed America.

Why? Because of something you guys will never understand. America isn't about a building or two, not about financial centers, not about military centers, America isn't about a place, and America isn't even about a bunch of bodies. America is about an IDEA. An idea that you can go someplace where you can earn as much as you can figure out how to, live for the most part like you envisioned living, and pursue happiness. (No guarantees that you'll reach it, but you can sure try!)

You guys seem to be incapable of understanding that we don't live in America, America lives in US! American Spirit is what it's called. And killing a few thousand of us, or a few million of us, won't change it. Most of the time, it's a pretty happy-go-lucky kind

of spirit. Until we're crossed in a cowardly manner—
then it becomes an entirely different kind of spirit.

Wait until you see what we do with that spirit
this time.

*

> *"It is such a privilege for us to perform for you
> tonight and to see you make a choice to come out, to
> laugh and most importantly to carry on and not be
> ruled by fear. Together we are all going to get
> through this and we are going to be OK."*

—VALERIE HARPER, ADDRESSING AUDI-
ENCES FOR THE BROADWAY COMEDY *The Tale
of the Allergist's Wife, Salon.com* 9/17/2001

*

FROM AN AOL POST, 9/16/2001 5:28 PM
EASTERN DAYLIGHT TIME
SUBJECT: STRONGER THAN YOU'LL EVER
KNOW

The beautiful country of America and its loyal citizens are stronger than anyone will ever know or
realize. People have tried and will probably continue

to try to knock our esteem and our power down, but no one has succeeded yet, and no one ever shall.

This week terrorists have only reminded us once again what living in America really means . . . standing by one another, respecting everyone in a time of need, and staying loyal to our country.

*

"Before a catastrophe, we can't imagine coping with the burdens that might confront us in a dire moment. Then, when that moment arrives, we suddenly find that we have resources inside us that we knew nothing about. What I've discovered is that we are able—all of us—to do much more than we think we can. Just look at me."

—CHRISTOPHER REEVE, ON BEARING UP
UNDER DURESS, *U.K. Telegraph* 9/27/2001

*

FROM AN AOL POST, 9/16/2001 2:29 PM
EASTERN DAYLIGHT TIME
SUBJECT: SCARED SILLY BUT STILL STRONG!

I'm 13, and when I heard about what happened in my 2nd period math class, I freaked. I live in Natick, Massachusetts, which has the 4th best Army labs in the whole country, so you can tell a lot of us kids were afraid of getting bombed because of it, but we are still alive and the point is we need to keep on going strong, don't let that light that all Americans have go out . . .

*

"Great men, great nations, have not been boasters and buffoons, but perceivers of the terror of life, and have manned themselves to face it."

—RALPH WALDO EMERSON,
The Conduct of Life

*

FROM AN AOL POST FROM A 16-YEAR-OLD FROM OHIO, 9/15/2001 2:11 PM EASTERN DAYLIGHT TIME
SUBJECT: MEMORY IN WORDS

We wake up tomorrow in a different world. But though our hearts are broken, we will not break down.

Though our tears are falling, we will not fall.

Though the fires have burned, our fire will not burn out.

Though we have lost, we are not lost.

We wake up tomorrow in a different world...

But we wake up...

And for that, we are thankful.

＊

"The markets open tomorrow, people go back to work, and we'll show the world."

—PRESIDENT GEORGE W. BUSH,
The New York Times 9/17/2001

＊

FROM AN AOL POST, 9/21/2001 5:36 PM
EASTERN DAYLIGHT TIME
SUBJECT: EVERYONE LISTEN TO ME, AND
QUIT YOUR BICKERING!!!

Before last Tuesday, we were living in a bubble that someone crashed a jet carrier into and burst. Now is this time for us to unite. Now is the time for race, religion, political party, ethnicity, and any other boundaries to be put away! We are Americans, and we should be standing up for our country.

The day the towers fell, American pride soared. Now we need to stand behind our leaders and use every ounce of patriotism we possess to support those who lead us. America will not fall, and American resolve is something that cannot be broken; it's stronger than steel or concrete. And it doesn't matter how many buildings fall; we will still be Americans and we will still have American pride.

> *"I wore this because we are going to rebuild. I wanted to drape my body in the America flag, is what I wanted to do."*
>
> —A MAN WEARING A T-SHIRT
> THAT READS "WE WILL REBUILD,"
> *The New York Times* 9/14/2001

You must have been very pleased Tuesday morning as you watched those planes slam into the towers. You must have felt great satisfaction as you watched the Pentagon burn. Images of men and women jumping to their deaths, of our grief and our horror, must have brought a smile to your face.

But you have not defeated us—look again:

Heroic firemen and policemen, running toward the flames, offering their lives to save strangers. Wounded men and women struggling to carry to safety someone they didn't even know. Bystanders ferrying wounded to hospitals in their own cars. Volunteers frantically trying to clear the rubble by hand, their fingers raw and bloody.

The horror and the carnage are your images.

The acts of heroism, of selflessness, of compassion and caring—those are our images, the images of America, of democracy and of freedom.

We will grieve, and we will be comforted. We will haul away your rubble and we will rebuild. We will turn your evil into resolve, and resolve into action. Like the mythological Phoenix, the towers will rise again from the ashes and the rubble that resulted from your unreasoning hatred.

"We have to express our grief and pause and say our prayers. But we also have to stay strong and we also have to continue with the search and rescue . . . And we have to send a clear message that New Yorkers aren't intimidated."

—GOVERNOR GEORGE PATAKI,
Newsday 9/13/2001

FROM AN AOL POST, 9/23/2001 8:16 PM
EASTERN DAYLIGHT TIME
SUBJECT: MORE AWARE OF MY SUR-
ROUNDINGS

Since the attacks on September 11 I have become very aware of what and who is around me.

As a flight attendant I rarely ever paid much attention to who boarded my flights. Now I seem to remember details. I remember the guy from two days ago in the emergency exit row wearing a blue shirt and the couple in first class who hugged me and thanked me for coming to work.

I have become a more positive person, and I now know that I can't take things for granted. So now I am enjoying every day to the fullest, I am flying three to four flights daily, and I am proud to be a flight attendant in the United States of America.

I wear a red, white, blue, and black ribbon every day to show how patriotic I am. I continue on with my life as normally as possible. And if I am one of those unfortunate ones to get laid off due to low passenger loads on my flights, I have already got the paperwork done to join the military and go fight for my country.

I will always be aware of my surroundings from this day forward, and will never look back and feel ashamed, because I know that what I do makes a difference to many people day after day.

❋

"When Tower 2 came down, we just started digging. We keep on going 'cause that's what we do."

—NEW YORK CITY FIREFIGHTER,
New York Magazine 9/24/2001

I drove to work today, and I served the public. I looked into the faces of the walking wounded, and I took my place among them again at the close of day.

I reassured people who said, "I feel so guilty for coming here to shop."

I touched their hand, and let them know that they were doing their part to keep the fabric of our society from falling apart.

Freedom is not just a word. It is a living, breathing concept that bin Laden can't understand. It resides in our soul, and is treasured from our mother's womb. He can't understand how we can go on with life in the face of such loss. He can't understand a nation that values Muslim Americans as he could never value them (as gracious, gentle people).

He doesn't see the shame he has brought to them . . . not because they are part of his fanatical cause (for they are not), but because his race is theirs, as Tim McVeigh's race was part of us.

Ashamed that a man of Islam could take something so holy and distort it, twist it, and mangle it as he did the structure of the WTC. Please remember that Islamic Americans are not to blame. See them, as we all are, as "members of the walking wounded."

"With malice toward none; with charity for all; with firmness in the right, as God gives us to see the right, let us strive on to finish the work we are in; to bind up the nation's wounds; to care for him who shall have borne the battle, and for his widow and his orphan—to do all which may achieve and cherish a just and lasting peace among ourselves and with all nations."

—ABRAHAM LINCOLN, SECOND
INAUGURAL ADDRESS, 3/4/1865

UNITED

"We've seen the unfurling of flags, the lighting of candles, the giving of blood, the saying of prayers in English, Hebrew, and Arabic. We have seen the decency of a loving and giving people who have made the grief of strangers their own. My fellow citizens, for the last nine days, the entire world has seen for itself the state of our Union, and it is strong."

—GEORGE W. BUSH, ADDRESS
TO A JOINT SESSION OF CONGRESS 9/17/2001

Over the past week I've heard a lot of people say "God Bless America." Every time someone says that I say to myself, "He already has."

I'm just 14, but I can see how God has blessed our great nation through this tragedy. First, he blessed us by making us a stronger nation. He brought us together. Through this terrible event he made us more united. When it looked like the terrorists had broken us, we stood behind our flag and before the world. We were united, along with our allies, under one common goal, to rid the world of evil. God has blessed us with an opportunity to do this.

Most of all, God blessed us with all the people lost. They have affected our lives whether we know it or not, and we thank God that we had a chance to know them, and we will miss them. Even though the horizon seems dark; the dust and ash will settle, and we will arise, a victorious nation. So when all hope seems lost, it's not.

God has given us so many blessings through this, and they're already noticeable today, but when our nerves settle, the blessings will shine through in splendid light.

FROM AN AOL POST, 9/14/2001 3:30 PM
EASTERN DAYLIGHT TIME
SUBJECT: A NATION RISES

Through the rubble, dust and blood
Together friends and strangers stood
Looking at each other, eye to eye
Not just people, rushing by

Stopping, helping, risking life
Caring not about meeting times
Looking not at race nor creed
Their only thought was those in need

Working side by side, brow to brow
Forgetting all but what is now
Digging in with all their might
Working hard, both day and night

As a nation united they take a stand
Helping each other, hand in hand
A nation bent, yet remaining strong
United together, standing tall

September eleventh, a nation fell
On that same day, it rose as well

"We Republicans and Democrats, House and Senate, stand strongly united behind the President, and we'll work together to ensure that the full resources of the government are brought to bear in these efforts."

—Senate majority leader Tom
Daschle, *The New York Times* 9/12/2001

The time is here for us to drop the hyphen and be American. Not African, not Irish, not Italian, or whatever kind of hyphenation that is put in front of "American" to show loyalty to one's roots.

The fact of the matter is that attack was on Americans, all of us, the African, the Irish, the Italian, and so on. Those hijackers did not give a damn about our hyphens.

I feel strange writing this because I'm a product of the 60s. Anyone who was a teenager then knows what I'm talking about. I've never been the flag-waving type and probably never will, but right here right now, I'm proud to be an American and from this day on I'll never refer to myself as an African-American again . . . I'm an AMERICAN.

I would like to send out my heartfelt condolences to the people of New York and Washington. I, along with millions of others, have watched in disbelief at what you have had to endure. I am just one person, of course, but I want to say how very proud you make me to be an American citizen.

I have heard my entire life that people living in New York, and certainly Washington, were pretty much cold, unfeeling people.

Nothing could be farther from the truth. I have watched with pride as you have helped each other and risked your lives for each other. I only hope I can come to your great and good part of the world one of these days and see for myself how you have rebuilt your cities and your lives.

Having lost my 17-year-old daughter in an automobile accident, I know the unbearable pain of losing a loved one. But let me tell you, I have never witnessed such dignity in despair. Thank you for restoring my faith in mankind. Especially in Americans.

> *"New York City & Washington, D.C.: Oklahoma cares. You stood with us in our darkest hour, now we stand with you."*

—FROM A FULL-PAGE STATEMENT SUBMITTED BY THE PEOPLE OF OKLAHOMA AND THE OKLAHOMA CITY NATIONAL MEMORIAL, *The New York Times* 9/13/2001

FROM AN AOL POST, 9/22/2001 12:59 AM
EASTERN DAYLIGHT TIME
SUBJECT: WHY DID WE HAVE TO WAIT
UNTIL NOW?

In the past ten days we have heard countless stories of this tragedy bringing out the best in the American people. Our country has united. You only need to look down the street and see all the flags hanging from porches and on poles. But why is it that we need to have something of this horrible magnitude happen before we stop worrying about what politician slept with whom?

I guarantee that the same transformation of the American people occurred when Pearl Harbor was bombed. But 60 years is a long time to remember, and most people had forgotten and gone back to worrying about things that don't really matter in the slightest.

Let's make sure that we don't forget this time, and keep what's important in a clear perspective from now on.

*

FROM AN AOL POST, 9/23/2001 3:00 PM
EASTERN DAYLIGHT TIME
SUBJECT: HOW THE TERRORISTS ARE WIN-
NING

If we don't stop hate crimes happening all across the U.S., the terrorists will win. Before September 11, 2001, people were French-American, Mexican-American, African-American, Polish-American, or Swiss-American, or whatever. Now they ALL are just American.

One of my friends is from Afghanistan, and her family was hurt in just the same way as everyone else. Just because they're Middle Eastern doesn't mean they did it or that they're all for bin Laden. One Middle Eastern man was KILLED in Arizona by some idiot calling himself a PATRIOT!

America is not about violence or hate! It's about freedom and certain inalienable rights: life, liberty, and the pursuit of happiness. That means stop the hatin'! We're all American, and we're in this together!

"We are caught in an inescapable network of mutuality, tied in a single garment of destiny. All life is interrelated."

—DR. MARTIN LUTHER KING, JR.,
"LETTER FROM BIRMINGHAM JAIL"

FROM AN AOL POST, 9/21/2001 10:24 AM
EASTERN DAYLIGHT TIME
SUBJECT: ONE NATION

When our country is attacked, we are not Catholic, Lutheran, Methodist, Muslim, Jewish or Buddhist, we are all Americans.

FROM AN AOL POST, 9/16/2001 8:36 AM
EASTERN DAYLIGHT TIME
SUBJECT: WE HAVE TO UNITE TO MAKE IT
THROUGH THIS TRAGEDY

As an African-American woman, I ask that we all put aside our differences of race, status, and sexual orientation and unite as Americans.

As an open hand we are weak, but as a fist we are strong.

✸

FROM AN AOL POST, 9/14/2001 2:41 AM
EASTERN DAYLIGHT TIME
SUBJECT: I WAS AT MY HOME SWEET
HOME

I was at home when I heard the news. My daughter called me from work. At that moment I felt that New York was right here in my home, as well as feeling that I was in New York.

✸

"No man is an island, entire of itself; every man is a piece of the continent."

—JOHN DONNE, "FOR WHOM THE BELL TOLLS"

FROM AN AOL POST, 9/15/2001 12:45 PM
EASTERN DAYLIGHT TIME
SUBJECT: WE ARE ONE

On that Tuesday, all Americans were New Yorkers and all humans were Americans.

"This is a crime against the foundations of our common humanity. Our response must be to stand shoulder to shoulder."

—PRESIDENT OF IRELAND MARY MCALEESE, *The New York Times* 9/12/2001

Thank you to all the foreigners who became one with us on September 11. I think we finally realized how to put all our differences aside and become one race, the human race.

I'm from New York, and my brother is a police officer. He was at his second job, or he would have been there helping before knowing the full toll. He did end up going there after work and did help pull a few broken hurting souls from that monstrous rubble.

Yesterday I heard someone call in to my radio station saying that the firefighters and police officers who risked their lives weren't heroes because they get paid to do it; therefore, it was their job. Where else do you see people delving into a wreckage that you know could kill them to pull out wounded souls? Where else do you toss aside your own safety, your own life to save the lives of others?

We have had many problems in New York with our police officers. I won't say no, but two days ago they were all heroes, every one of them. I want to thank them as well.

I want to thank the newscasters who haven't once

said "I can't go there, I'll be hurt," but took us straight there to help us bear witness to the cruelty of those faceless, masked people. And bearing witness is important so that we never forget and never let it happen again.

Two days ago we lost our innocence, our belief that we were safe and untouchable, and, in some ways, our freedom. Yet we gained togetherness, we gained appreciation of our police and buildings, we gained family—New York, America, and the world gathered together and became a family.

*

> *"The salvation of mankind lies only in making everything the concern of all."*
>
> —ALEXANDER SOLZHENITSYN,
>   NOBEL LECTURE, 1970

*

FROM AN AOL POST, 9/14/2001 7:02 PM
EASTERN DAYLIGHT TIME
SUBJECT: GOD BLESS

Watching TV Tuesday morning and seeing plane number one hit the first tower, I actually thought it was an accident. Until plane number two came along. When I saw the second plane hit, all my thoughts just went blank. I have never felt so sad in my life. All I could think was "God, please help us."

Our home was destroyed in a matter of minutes. Everything we know was taken away from us, but everything at the same time was gained. We all pulled together, from firefighters to police officers, from volunteers to hotline staffers. We will pull through this and we will win at the end.

I have never been so proud to be an American. May God help us and may God forgive the ones that do not know any better.

*

"'And kill not that which Allah has held sacred.' May Allah expose the wrong doers and bring them to justice, no matter who they are."

—FROM A SIGN ON A MOSQUE DOOR QUOTING THE KORAN, *New York Magazine* 9/24/2001

*

FROM AN AOL POST, 9/15/2001 1:21 AM
EASTERN DAYLIGHT TIME
SUBJECT: MY SYMPATHIES ARE WITH YOU

Tonight, as a Friday night Jimtown High School football game started, the firefighters of Baugo Township in Elkhart, Indiana, brought the flag out and put it up. And as the high school choir sang and the band played and the director played taps and the flag was raised to half-staff, people in the bleachers were only thinking of how something this horrible could possibly happen to the United States.

"USA" was written out on the field in red, white, and blue, and at the end of the memorial, red, white, and blue balloons were released into the air, and we had a moment of silence for the lives lost due to terrorism.

Everyone has felt the impact of this, and all I can say is that everyone across the country is really showing how united we are.

FROM AN AOL POST, 9/16/2001 7:37 PM
EASTERN DAYLIGHT TIME
SUBJECT: AN AMERICAN HEART

We feel the pain, we feel the sorrow. We see a nation on its knees, united and crying for an answer. No, there is not a right answer, there are no words that can describe the pain.

I was not born in this land, but I became an American citizen by choice, because I love this land, this country. I just want to pass the word that when you become a citizen of a country by choice you do so out of love. I love the people, the culture, the history. I love you, and today I pray that God gives me the wisdom to share with people that not all foreigners can harm America.

＊

FROM AN AOL POST, 9/17/2001 8:33 PM
EASTERN DAYLIGHT TIME
SUBJECT: I AM FROM SINGAPORE

I moved to live in the U.S.A. with my family a couple of years ago. I lived a sheltered life in the small island of Singapore and was just about to feel being at home in the U.S. My heart broke for America as I watched the news coverage on TV.

I am also touched beyond words as I observed Americans coming together in rescue efforts, to support each other and mourn their loss. I am glad I will have an opportunity to be one of you . . . one day.

*

"My country is the world, and my religion is to do good."

—THOMAS PAINE, *The Age of Reason*

*

FROM AN AOL POST, 9/15/2001 7:23 PM
EASTERN DAYLIGHT TIME
SUBJECT: HOW MANY PRAYERS?

How many prayers for the mothers searching for their children, the daughters looking for their fathers, all the friends who are missing?

How many prayers for the multitude of rescue workers, the countless people still unaccounted for, the unknown buried beneath debris?

How many prayers for the faceless bodies pulled out of the rubble, the unidentified screams of a few helpless survivors, the unanswered cell phone calls from the inside?

How many prayers for the innocent people who will never come home, the bodies flying out of the 85th-story windows like drifting sheets of paper, the witnesses from several blocks away?

How many prayers for the rejoicing Palestinians, the Middle Eastern immigrants being harassed in America, the Arab men being held as suspects?

How many prayers will bring them all back, rebuild the towers, return the feeling of safety to our home?

Are there enough prayers to restore all of the lost lives, to replace the fallen buildings, and to avoid this war against terrorism?

God, hear our many prayers today, and please, God bless America.

＊

FROM AN AOL POST, 9/14/2001 12:47 PM
EASTERN DAYLIGHT TIME
SUBJECT: THE WORLD IS UNITING

The only light that shines out of this terrible darkness is that people around the world are uniting and revering life again. Life is something that every single one of us has taken for granted. People everywhere are changed, and hopefully we'll all stop bickering about the petty things.

It warms my heart to see peoples and cultures that historically haven't been very fond of America have empathized and care about life. Having lived in Moscow, I've felt the anti-Americanism. But seeing that the Russians are having memorials and genuinely shedding tears for our losses encourages me and puts faith back in me that humans are capable of loving—no matter the color of their skin, the language they speak, or the religion they practice.

I also have a renewed sense of patriotism. I had lost it for quite some time as I sunk deeper into a cynical state. But my heart is full and proud to be a national of a country of such amazing, caring people. Not only have I shed tears of sadness, but also tears of joy to see so many Americans from every corner of this vast country donating blood, donating food, donating money, and donating their own lives to help others in such a time of tragedy. We all have so many differences, yet that makes us even more special.

I have never felt so much love for so many people and I want to let everyone know that you all have a piece of my heart. Let's remain this way—united and loving.

*"I will plant companionship thick as trees along all
the rivers of America,
And along the shores of the great lakes, and all
over the prairies,
I will make inseparable cities with their arms about
each other's necks."*

—WALT WHITMAN, "SONG OF MYSELF"

FROM AN AOL POST, 9/14/2001 6:02 AM
EASTERN DAYLIGHT TIME
SUBJECT: FROM GREAT BRITAIN

To America and her people . . .

Although a simple message may not be of any significant help or comfort to you at the moment, I want you all to know that the people of Great Britain are shocked and disgusted at what has happened to your nation.

You all have our greatest sympathies and support. Rest assured that the people and government of Great Britain are behind you 100 percent.

"In sorrow and sympathy with the U.S.A. You supported us in two world wars and more, and we stand with you now."

—FROM A CARD OUTSIDE THE U.S. EMBASSY IN LONDON, *The New York Times* 9/14/2001

"Canadians share the loss of loved ones and friends. On Friday our nation mourned with you for the victims of the terrorist attacks. We share your outrage, grief, compassion and resolve. The people of Canada are with you every step of the way. As friends. As neighbors. As family."

—FROM A FULL-PAGE AD IN *The New York Times* 9/17/2001

FROM AN AOL POST, 9/20/2001 8:24 PM
EASTERN DAYLIGHT TIME
SUBJECT: A LETTER TO THE TERRORISTS

Last Thursday night when my family went outside to light the candles for these wonderful heroes we lost, I was amazed that in a neighborhood where I had lived for two years and only met three or four of my neighbors, we filled my friends' front yard with over fifty people from our street. These were people of all ages, races, and religions, but we are all Americans. We came together as a neighborhood, the way this country will come together.

*

"These unspeakable acts have shattered our City and shocked our nation. But they have not weakend the bonds that unite us as New Yorkers, as Americans—as those who love freedom—and, ultimately, as those who love one another. Our strength will defeat this evil. Our spirit will overcome this atrocity. And, together, this land of people, and by the people, will soar higher than even our beloved twin towers."

— GOVERNOR GEORGE E. PATAKI,
SPEECH TO THE JOINT SESSION OF THE NEW
YORK STATE LEGISLATURE 9/13/2001

*

I have few words to say compared to the tremendous well of emotion in my heart. All I can think about is the victims, their families, the rescuers lost, and our country on bended knee. My prayers are the only comfort . . . my blood and money, my only offering . . . my tears, the only expression these days . . . and my hope, the only thing that keeps me going.

We are a family . . . every one of us. Even though we may have never met . . . we are bound together by our citizenship and our patriotism.

Our skin color does not matter, or our religion. We are Americans. And we cry together . . . as one.

My hope is that we will remain united. That we will treat our neighbors and our children with care and compassion. The man who prays differently than me, the one I've seen a hundred times a week, the citizen of the same, great country as me, the man with an accent . . . darker skin, ethnic clothing—that man is flying our flag as proudly as you and me. He weeps as you and I have and does not deserve the rock through his window or the names we call his children all of a sudden. We are better than this kind of ignorance displayed recently . . .

For God's sake . . . WE ARE AMERICANS, a nation built on diversity and freedom of speech, religion, and opinions. My hope is that we come out of this with a greater sense of compassion to our fellow human beings—that we can transcend not only the tragedy of death but celebrate life.

My hope is that we unite and stay that way . . . shoulder to shoulder with our fellow Americans, and wave this beautiful flag . . . together.

There has been enough devastation to last 100 lifetimes, let's not create more in our own backyard. John Lennon said it best . . . Love is all you need.

*

> *"We have learned that we cannot live alone, at peace: that our own well-being is dependent on the well-being of other nations, far away. We have learned that we must live as men, and not as ostriches, nor as dogs in the manger. We have learned to be citizens of the world, members of the human community."*
>
> —FRANKLIN DELANO ROOSEVELT,
> FOURTH INAUGURAL ADDRESS, 1/20/1945

RESOURCEFUL

"These are the times that try man's souls."

—THOMAS PAINE, *The American Crisis*

FROM AN AOL POST, 9/15/2001 5:41 PM
EASTERN DAYLIGHT TIME
SUBJECT: MANY MODEST HEROES IN
              TIMES OF TRAGEDY

Tuesday morning I was getting ready for work and watching the "Today" show when the second plane hit the WTC. I was stunned and brought to tears, as were many Americans both near and far.

That night, as my husband came home from

work, he called to tell me there was a man standing on an overpass near Castle Rock, Colorado, waving a large American flag at the evening traffic. I immediately and most proudly went out and flew the Stars and Stripes at our house.

This wonderful man continued this vigil daily; three days later, a local news crew went out to cover the awesome scene—his bicentennial flag waving and hundreds of motorists honking in appreciation.

This modest man in his late 50s simply said that this was his job today. He could not fight for his country anymore, he said, but he could do this. At one point, a local sheriff's deputy pulled up next to him and he thought he would be told to go home. Instead, the deputy shook his hand and thanked him.

The fortitude shown by this one man touched the hearts of hundreds of people in southern Colorado, just as that of the rescue workers, Americans joining in prayer, and the loved ones who search tirelessly for friends and family in the city of New York touch all of us.

I have noticed too that in small ways Americans are making an effort to be connected to one another once again. When I went to the grocery store last night, I noticed that an unusual number of strangers were making eye contact with one another, going out of their way to hold doors for one another, and simply smiling and saying hello.

This is again the America of my youth. The one where we all joined together in saying the pledge of allegiance and no voice was silent.

Thank you to the people of this country and its quietly modest heroes who make it great. Thank you for restoring our faith in humanity and helping to lessen our sorrow. Thank you to those who choose to do small things that make a difference to so many!

*

"It is not in the still calm of life, or in the repose of a pacific station, that great characters are formed. . . . The habits of a vigorous mind are formed in contending with difficulties. All history will convince you of this, and that wisdom and penetration are the fruit of experience, not the lessons of retirement and leisure. Great necessities call out great virtues."

—ABIGAIL ADAMS, LETTER TO JOHN
QUINCY ADAMS

*

FROM AN AOL POST, 9/25/2001 12:55 PM
EASTERN DAYLIGHT TIME
SUBJECT: THIS IS HOW I'M GOING TO
HELP

Yesterday, I contacted the NYPD and gave them my support in the form of translation services. I speak fluent Arabic. I will translate documents they intercept and even spy on Arab conversations if necessary.

I love America. I only wish I could have used my skills sooner.

＊

"The Parks Department sent over six big light towers usually used for outdoor concerts so we could keep digging at night."

—RESCUE WORKER, *Newsday* 9/13/2001

＊

The fact that so many people offer support with both their time and money is extremely important and is greatly appreciated (beyond mere words).

But the simplest and perhaps most helpful thing to do is to listen to others who have been impacted by this atrocity. Offer your emotional support. If you know someone who was there and survived, or if you know someone who is wondering about someone who they cannot find, or if someone has found out that a loved one is no longer with them . . . LISTEN or at least check in to find out how they are faring emotionally.

Let people talk . . . But more so let them know you are really there for them . . . Let them know their lives and those of their loved ones are valuable to you. We all want to feel loved and appreciated. Unfortunately, many of us do not feel that way on a regular basis.

I was actually at Ground Zero when the first plane struck the tower. I am incredibly lucky and fortunate to have survived with just a concussion, a few scrapes, bruises, and a swollen leg dodging the concrete falling at my head. The fact that I am holding my own and am relatively calm on the outside does not mean that I am okay on the inside. The physical pain is nothing compared to the emotional pain.

That's how you can help . . . Listen and care about people around you . . . It's simple and priceless.

*

FROM AN AOL POST, 9/14/2001 10:26 PM
EASTERN DAYLIGHT TIME

I am an employee of K-Sea Transportation (a tug and barge company in Staten Island, New York.

I am proud to say that K-Sea jumped right into the rescue effort as soon as the tragedy happened. We sent tugs to assist in moving persons from New York to ports of New Jersey, etc. We sent a water barge to New York to help in supplying water for cleanup, showers, and drinking water for all workers and military vessels.

I am also a very grateful employee because my daughter was trapped in downtown Manhattan that awful day with no way out of the city—and K-

Sea sent a tug just to find her. I know how much time and money it costs to send a tug to go up and down the piers of NYC, and I am so grateful and happy to say they found my daughter and returned her to me untouched by the traumatic hours others had to endure to get safely out of that madness.

***

> "Everybody that has a boat in the water is trying to help out, taking passengers to Hoboken, doing what we can."

— NEW YORK FERRY CAPTAIN,
The New York Times 9/12/2001

***

FROM AN AOL POST, 9/15/2001 7:06 AM
EASTERN DAYLIGHT TIME
SUBJECT: HELPING TEENS COPE WITH
             FEELINGS CONCERNING THE
             TRAGEDY

I am an art teacher in a school in Southwest Florida. As Tuesday's tragedy unfolded, I could see that my day's art lesson plan needed an immediate alteration. After consulting my principal, I greeted the sixth-, seventh-, and eighth-grade drawing classes with pencils and paper—the kind that is used in kindergarten, with lines on the bottom half and a blank space at the top.

While the TV continued to report the devastating news, I explained through my tears that we, as artists, could visually record an event and also let out our feelings through our drawings. I went on to explain that we could also write whatever we want on the paper. I told them about Picasso, and how he painted the wall-sized "Guernica" to visually portray the horrors of the war in Spain.

They immediately started writing and drawing. Some wrote prayers, stories, one line of feelings, or nothing at all. I also used this lesson with the next morning's class. The drawings and the writings were so heartfelt that I faxed some to the local newspaper, which immediately came out and took photos of some of the students and their drawings and interviewed me.

I did this little "art therapy" lesson with 57 students and I only hope that in a small way, my students could cope with all that was happening.

✹

"We've been forming carpools at the rental counter since the airports are shut down. They say that people work together in times of crisis."

—A STRANDED TRAVELER IN DETROIT,
The New York Times 9/12/2001

FROM AN AOL POST, 9/14/2001 12:32 PM
EASTERN DAYLIGHT TIME
SUBJECT: HELPING IN KANSAS

The city of Leavenworth had a blood drive today. I arrived 30 minutes after they opened to find that they had already moved to the gym due to the large response. After waiting for 2 hours, the staff said it would be an additional 4- to 5-hour wait and that they would stay late to continue taking blood.

Instead of getting upset, people kept coming. The Red Cross said they would be doing special blood drives for the next 4 to 5 weeks to help our country. I know that this isn't a lot, but it just goes to show how this country has banded together as one.

In Kansas City, the firefighters just had their annual donation drive.

Today, they were out again, asking for donations to send to those in need. No one asked them, they just did it.

✳

"We didn't have any tables, so we put bagels and granola bars out on stretchers for the emergency service workers."

—VOLUNTEER AT CHELSEA PIERS,
The New York Times 9/14/2001

✳

FROM AN AOL POST, 9/14/2001 3:24 PM
EASTERN DAYLIGHT TIME
SUBJECT: DOWN THE ROAD

A friend of my son was not fortunate enough to have his daddy come home the other night, and as a New Jersey parent, I have been struggling to determine what I can do to help. The blood banks are turning people away, as are the local shelters, which are overwhelmed with supplies . . . so several of us at school have already decided that we will hold a blood drive in six months to honor the victims of this horrible tragedy.

My only hope is that people do not forget, and that the same support is evident then as well . . . we will do our part at least to ensure that this community never forgets.

❋

FROM AN AOL POST, 9/16/2001 5:16 PM
EASTERN DAYLIGHT TIME
SUBJECT: MAKING SANDWICHES

I am a student at New York University in New York City. Today, a few of my soccer teammates and I made more than 3,000 sandwiches for the rescue workers risking their lives. I am glad I could help.

❋

"Give us the tools, and we will finish the job."

—WINSTON CHURCHILL,
RADIO BROADCAST, 2/9/1941

❋

FROM AN AOL POST, 9/25/2001 8:34 PM
EASTERN DAYLIGHT TIME
SUBJECT: MY 10-YEAR-OLD

My 10-year-old daughter and her friends made keychains. We took them to a local storefront and asked for donations for the September 11 fund. At the end of the day they collected over a thousand dollars. We are doing it again this weekend.

I can't ever remember feeling this sad or helpless. This was good therapy for us as well as our children.

FROM AN AOL POST, 9/23/2001 10:40 PM
EASTERN DAYLIGHT TIME
SUBJECT: THE WALL: HOW MY SCHOOL
RAISED MONEY

My club, Students Against Drunk Driving, sold red, white, and blue paper bricks (which were all donated by Office Max and Office Depot) for a dollar apiece. For every dollar donated, people signed their name onto a piece of paper that stated "I'm Rebuilding America."

We raised $1,000 in a week! And this is a high school! It's all going to the Red Cross relief fund!

FROM AN AOL POST, 9/15/2001 6:31 PM
EASTERN DAYLIGHT TIME
SUBJECT: HAD TO SHARE THIS DAY

Yesterday my mom called me at work and said she was getting so many calls at the Red Cross office asking what people could do to help and where they could come donate. She asked if I could set something up for this weekend, so I called Wal-Mart, which donated space and volunteers.

I then went to places like video stores, restaurants, and Pepsi-Cola, asking for things we could give to those who came and gave money. Every single one of them gave; even Papa John's pizza delivered us pizzas every hour to give away.

I saw the most incredible outpouring of generosity I have ever seen in my life. People actually handed us $50 bills just for a bag of popcorn; another gave us $100 and just asked for a red, white, and blue ribbon. I saw young and old, black, white, Indian, and even people of Arabic descent searching their wallets for money to give.

I was in tears more than once today.

Somebody thought that by flying airplanes into our buildings they could tear apart this nation; what they did was bring it together even stronger. I haven't done the final count yet, but the last we counted we had made over $2,000, and we will be back out tomorrow.

***

FROM AN AOL POST, 9/16/2001 12:18 AM
EASTERN DAYLIGHT TIME
SUBJECT: HOW OUR SCHOOL HELPED . . .

I'm a senior at the Ethel Walker School in Connecticut. One day every week we will cut down on our lunch costs and eat broth, rice, and oranges in remembrance of those that were lost in this great tragedy.

The $400 we save on each meal when we do this is sent to various organizations and hospitals that are in need of such funds. I urge others to think of such sacrifices that they could observe and also help those in need.

If there was ever a time to be proud of your country and of your fellow Americans, it is now . . .

*

"Necessity is the mother of courage, as of invention."

—WALTER SCOTT, *Quentin Durward*, 1823

*

FROM AN AOL POST, 9/14/2001 6:10 PM
EASTERN DAYLIGHT TIME
SUBJECT: FOOD TOUR!

I am the manager of a mobile marketing tour. We were working in the Boston market when the WTC was hit. The feeling of helplessness was so heavy.

On Wednesday we were contacted by the client, who told us to drop what we were doing in Boston and head for New York to see if we could help. We are currently serving hot plates of food to the relief workers at ground zero.

*

FROM AN AOL POST, 9/14/2001 7:11 PM
EASTERN DAYLIGHT TIME
SUBJECT: CHILDREN CAN HELP

I am a teacher in Buffalo, New York. Today all of our public school children wore red, white, and blue. We had a moment of silence to honor the dead.

And we collected new socks for the rescue workers.

The children wrote messages of hope in the socks, and a local church transported them to the rescue workers.

Our little school collected 200 pairs. It's a little thing but the kids understand how clean, dry socks might help a worker feel better. They felt proud to help.

PATRIOTIC

"Beneath Heaven's gracious will
The stars of progress still
Our course do sway;
In unity sublime
To broader heights we climb,
Triumphant over Time,
God speeds our way!"

—KATHARINE LEE BATES,
"AMERICA THE BEAUTIFUL"

What is America?

On September 11, 2001, the World Trade Center and the Pentagon were hit by American planes hijacked by terrorists. Buildings so large they each had their own Zip codes were destroyed, and thousands of people were murdered. Headlines around the world read "Attack on America."

But was America attacked? What is America?

America is

Many victims calling their families and friends to say, "No matter what happens to me, I love you."

America is

Hundreds of firefighters and paramedics arriving within minutes, putting their own lives in jeopardy, to help thousands of victims escape burning buildings.

America is

While the second Trade Center building began to burn, nearby priests ran to the scene to give last rites to victims in their final moments.

America is

People running down flight after flight of stairs,

and two women stopping to carry a disabled co-worker down 68 flights.

America is

Shoe merchants throwing shoes and slippers to barefoot strangers and women wearing high heels so they could run a little faster from the tumbling buildings.

America is

U.S. servicemen and women at the Pentagon protecting their country as flames loomed over their heads.

America is

In perhaps the most courageous act of democracy ever, passengers aboard United Airlines flight 93 voting to try to overthrow their hijackers after hearing that two other planes had hit the World Trade Center. They knew that although they would surely perish, they would save more lives on the ground.

America is

Millions of Americans watching the news as it unfolded and praying to G-d to help the victims escape quickly and to ask that lives be spared.

America is

Hundreds of emergency personnel staying to help out "just one more person" as the buildings crumbled.

America is

Restaurant owners and New Yorkers bringing water, coffee, and food to workers who tirelessly toiled to find survivors. As each left to be replaced by a rested colleague, New Yorkers cheered them and thanked them.

America is

Lines three or four hours long at blood banks across the country, many having to turn people away.

America is

Millions of homes displaying American flags sending out messages of love and hope to the thousands of victims and their families. Within hours, millions of flags disappeared off store shelves, and many more were back-ordered.

America is

Doctors, nurses, counselors, and firefighters arriving from many other neighboring states, leaving their homes and jobs at a moment's notice, asking how they can help.

America is

A young Russian-born man meeting an elderly Jewish woman frantically looking for her husband among the debris. The young man spent the next two days helping her find him, so that they may spend their final days together.

America is

A young Pakistani-American NYU college student, after witnessing it all, lining up to give blood, offering water to relief workers, and praying to Allah to return peace to his country.

America is

Jewish families calling their fellow Muslim-American neighbors and asking if they are okay and if anyone in their family was affected by the tragedy. They offered each other their support in the weeks and months ahead.

America is

Stranded travelers renting campers, U-Hauls, taxicabs, and rental cars, asking complete strangers if they wanted rides to other states to be with their loved ones.

America is

Prayer services, open to the public, taking place in every town, in every city, in every state in the entire nation. Millions of candles were lit in remembrance of the victims. People prayed in churches, synagogues, temples, mosques, and houses of worship in hundreds of faiths, in dozens of languages. Priests stood with rabbis, ministers, reverends, imams, Christian Science readers, and other spiritual leaders, praying together to the same G-d. Together they prayed for all Americans, and for peace in the world.

America is

Catholic and Protestant Irish-Americans working together on bake sales, car washes, and pancake breakfasts to raise money for the Red Cross Disaster Relief Fund.

America is

Millions of schoolchildren in thousands of cities writing cards and drawing pictures to be sent to New York and Washington, D.C.

America is

Construction workers all over the country painting American flags on building roofs so that pilots overhead know they are valued and appreciated.

America is

Politicians who previously battled their political opponents with great fervor hugging them, crying with them, and sitting with them at memorial services.

America is

Investors all over the world saying, "As a sign of my support for America, I will believe in the strength of the United States and its ability to recover. I will invest in the American spirit."

America is

Teachers in thousands of schools wiping tears, calming fears, and reminding their students that while the war is on terrorism, the enemy is hate.

America is

Millions of people from dozens of faiths and hundreds of homelands standing together, unwilling to give up on their ideals of peace, justice, and brotherhood.

Did terrorists attack America? They attacked our buildings, they crashed our planes, and they killed many of our brothers and sisters. But did they attack America? No—they cannot. As long as there are people in need, and people who care, regardless of their backgrounds, we will always have America.

"For us, patriotism is the same as the love of humanity."

—MAHATMA GANDHI

America . . . the U.S.A. . . . Land of the free and home of the brave? My whole life I've questioned what America stood for—people fighting, killing, racism, and small "wars" with your own people. But this past week, I've been truly proud to be an American. Watching all these people rally together and become all of a sudden so patriotic has touched my heart in a way no one has before. I'm still young, 21, and I never imagined seeing something like this happen, let alone my kids seeing it.

I have two little girls, twins. They are 4 years old, and yesterday when they asked me, "Why did God let so many people die?" my eyes just filled up with tears.

What do you tell your kids when asked such a question?

I sat them down, and looked them in the eye and said, "God was with those people the whole way, He held on to them in their moment of need, and made sure that their wings were waiting for them the minute they entered heaven."

I told them that God was in the buildings, on the planes, and with the rescue workers, but God is also with every family of all the victims.

My two little girls still didn't seem to understand. Last night while tucking them in, I thought about the mother on the plane with her two little girls taking them on vacation, and I wondered what did she say to them, while on the plane, and how can a mother justify to her young children what happened. And I broke down, crying for all the families of victims and everyone this has affected.

My faith was restored when one of my daughters knocked on my door and climbed into my lap in her little nightgown. She was holding something. Before I could ask what it was, her sister came in, too. She too was holding something in her little hand. Each of them at the same time opened their hands, and they were both holding ten-dollar bills, their leftover birthday money.

One said, "Mommy, I want you to send this to people that need it, because if God would have taken you or daddy, I would want people to give me their birthday money too."

My other daughter gave me her ten dollars and said, "Mommy, I'm glad that God was with those people, they probably weren't so scared, knowing that He was holding them."

And the girls jumped to the floor and left the room. Right then I knew that this nation will come together, and one day we will mend hearts, and move on, with a new sense of pride. I took my daughters' donation to the Red Cross, and with it they asked me to write a note for them, and this is what is said:

Dear people,

My mommy says that God was with everyone who was hurt, and I'm glad because God makes everything better, and here is our birthday money, please use it to help kids find their mommies and daddies. P.S. God Bless America.

*

"Donating what we can just shows a sense of pride in the country."

—VOLUNTEER LOADING UP A RENTED VAN
WITH SUPPLIES, *Newsday* 9/17/2001

*

I am an American by choice, not by birth. I chose to become an American citizen because I admired its freedom, its democracy, and its people. I learned here that this, the greatest country in the world, might not have a perfect history, and that it still may have a way to go before perfect justice serves all. But I knew too that we Americans are trying, and trying hard, to correct past mistakes and avoid new ones.

I knew all that with my brain: that is why I became an American citizen. On September 11, I found that I have become an American by heart, too.

I felt the pain of my homeland down in my guts. I cried just by listening to "God Bless America." I stood proud of my countrymen and women. I am full of rage and hatred against those who dare to desecrate our land, and to murder my brothers and my sisters.

Thanks, America, for giving me a home. Thanks, America, for the heroism of your children. I, too, am willing to give my life for you.

"I want to pull over and cry. I love this country. America tried to help everybody. God bless America."

—A TAXI DRIVER FROM EGYPT,
The New York Times 9/12/2001

FROM AN AOL POST, 9/23/2001 4:17 PM
EASTERN DAYLIGHT TIME
SUBJECT: WHAT GENERATION X NEVER
UNDERSTOOD

I am a college student at the University of Georgia. I wrote this letter to my grandfather, who is a U.S. Army veteran, after the tragedy on 9-11-01. I want to dedicate it to all those who have served in our military, to those who continue to serve, and to those who will serve in the future. I will let the letter speak for itself.

Granddad,

There are a few things that I have been feeling this week that I would like to share with you. Until this unfortunate tragedy, I do not think the young people of America had any concept of war. In my short 21 years of life, I have always felt safe, never even considering threats from the outside world. I believed that my country was so strong that we were untouchable, but this week has proved different.

It has been the topic of discussion in all of my classes the entire week, and the same subject keeps coming up. Our generation really is clueless about how it must have been to live through what our grandparents, and even some of our parents have lived through, and for the first time, we are aware of our ignorance.

I don't think any history book will ever be able to help someone relive the feelings that I, and the rest of my fellow American citizens, are feeling at this moment. I suppose this is how you feel about the things you have seen throughout your life, and the wars you have been through.

For all the times I asked you about the wars, I was fascinated by what you were saying, but I never understood the true meaning of war. Stories can be told all day long, but this experience has given me a new perspective on the past.

I just want to tell you that for the first time I feel like I really appreciate what you did when you fought for our freedom in the war. I am so ashamed that it took something like this to make me realize what true heroes you and the rest of the armed forces really are. Before this tragedy I took my freedom for granted, but now that someone has threatened my freedom, I thank God for it every day.

I know that without you and all those who went to war for us in the past, I would not have the opportunities that I have now. I thank you for fighting for our country. You are a true hero, and I just wanted to tell you that.

*

"An incident like this brings out the patriotism in a person—it's a combination of anger at the people who attacked us and sadness for the people who've lost their lives."

—A MAN WEARING RED, WHITE, AND BLUE
RIBBONS ON THE LAPEL OF HIS JACKET,
Entertainment Weekly 9/28/2001

*

FROM AN AOL POST, 9/16/2001 8:03 PM
EASTERN DAYLIGHT TIME
SUBJECT: THE RAINBOW

On Friday night, Sept. 14 at 6:53 PM, I was riding through Rockland, Mass., and the most beautiful rainbow was in the sky. I hadn't seen one in years. It brought me to a church parking lot, where people had been gathering.

A woman asked if I would like to light a candle with them. I did. We prayed and then sang "My Country 'Tis of Thee." I was overcome by sadness.

As I rode home, the streets were lined with people holding candles and flags. I have never been prouder to be an American. My blessings go out to everyone who has been affected by this both directly and indirectly and God bless all the heroes who have so relentlessly volunteered their time and efforts towards this horrible tragedy. Let us continue to unite. We all need each other.

FROM AN AOL POST, 9/16/2001 5:01 PM
EASTERN DAYLIGHT TIME
SUBJECT: THE DAY I BECAME AN AMERI-
CAN

I was born in America in 1968, but I became an American on Sept. 11, 2001!

*

"These states are the amplest poem,
Here is not merely a nation but a teeming Nation of
  nations,
Here the doings of men correspond with the broad-
  cast doings
of the day and night,
Here is what moves in magnificent masses careless
  of particulars,
. . . Here the flowing trains, here the crowds, equal-
  ity, diversity, the soul loves."

—WALT WHITMAN, FROM "BY BLUE
  ONTARIO SHORE," *Leaves of Grass*

*

FROM AN AOL POST, 9/14/2001 12:36 AM
EASTERN DAYLIGHT TIME
SUBJECT: AT A VA HOSPITAL IN NORTH
CAROLINA

On September 11 I was at the Veterans Administration Hospital at Asheville, North Carolina. I am a disabled veteran, and I have to tell you—there was enough anger at the VA that if it could be turned into electricity it could have lit the world for the remainder of this century.

✹

"My neighbors painted their picket fence in red, white and blue."

—A woman in Atlanta, Georgia,
The New York Times 9/17/2001

✹

FROM AN AOL POST, 9/14/2001 8:52 PM
EASTERN DAYLIGHT TIME
SUBJECT: MY PRAYERS ARE WITH YOU

I have a son in the Marine Corps who may have to go to war. I'm proud to be his mother, and I'm proud that he represents our country.

If I could take his place, I would; if I could walk beside him in this, I would.

Let us pray for our military men and women who will serve our country, and let's pray they all come back home safely.

✳

"Patriotism depends as much on mutual suffering as on mutual success, and it is by that experience of all fortunes and all feelings that a great national character is created."

—BENJAMIN DISRAELI, SPEECH IN THE
HOUSE OF COMMONS, 3/18/1862

✳

In the wake of September 11, a day which Americans both old and young will remember, I have two types of tears.

My first tears are for all the families that lost their loved ones, friends that lost their loved ones, and for all of America, which has to face this tragic loss of life and the attack on our freedom.

And yet, in the midst of all this, I also have a different type of tears that I face every day. The tears of pride when I look around and see our "Old Glory" flying proud, the many heroes that are aiding in the search and rescue efforts, and the way people are standing united. And yes, the tears of pride when I scroll through all the touching thoughts and feelings that all you great people have shared.

Let us show that "they" have not broken our spirit.

*

"A thoughtful mind, when it sees a Nation's flag, sees not the flag only, but the Nation itself; and

*whatever may be its symbols, its insignia, he reads
chiefly in the flag the government, the principles,
the truths, the history which belongs to the nation
that sets it forth."*

—HENRY WARD BEECHER, FROM "THE
AMERICAN FLAG"

FROM AN AOL POST, 9/17/2001 10:18 PM
EASTERN DAYLIGHT TIME
SUBJECT: HOMETOWN FLAGS ARE EVERY-
WHERE!

Folks—
   A year ago, if you saw someone flying a flag on
their pickup truck, a lot of people would have said,
"There goes an extremist." Now, it's a different
story.

   I've seen all ethnicities, young and old, flying
flags on their SUVs, old pickup trucks, and Cadil-
lacs. Every town I've been through has more flags
than fire hydrants. I like what I'm seeing, and it is
contagious. Please, for our country's sake, keep this
spirit alive. It is going to take many battles and lots
of time to win this war. It's going to get to a point

where it will be convenient to slip back into that comfort zone we were all so used to. BUT DON'T. Patriotism is a life attitude, it is esprit de corps, it is remembrance, it is diligence, it is American.

Patriotism is all these things, but there is one thing it is not. It is not free. It comes with a cost. My fellow Americans, it is time to step back in time, reach down, pick up Old Glory from our fallen soldiers at the Chosin reservoir, Chapultepec, Antietam, Saigon, Guadalcanal, Iwo Jima— and continue to march!

*

> *"Each man must for himself alone decide what is right and what is wrong, which course is patriotic and which isn't. You cannot shirk this and be a man."*
>
> —MARK TWAIN

RESOLUTE

FROM AN AOL POST, 9/21/2001 12:04 AM
EASTERN DAYLIGHT TIME
SUBJECT: THE PILOT ON THE PLANE

This is something I received from a friend:

I just wanted to let you know that I arrived safe and sound into Dulles Airport tonight [9/15] at about 6:00. It was an interesting flight.

The airport in Denver was almost spooky, it was so empty and quiet. No one was in line for the security checkpoint when I got there, so that went fairly quickly, just x-ray of my bags and then a chemical test to be sure nothing explosive was on them.

Then I waited 2½ hours to board the plane.

What happened after we boarded was interesting, and I thought I would share it with you.

The pilot/captain came on the loudspeaker after the doors were closed.

His speech went like this:

"First, I want to thank you for being brave enough to fly today. The doors are now closed, and we have no help from the outside for any problems that might occur inside this plane. As you could tell when you checked in, the government has made some changes to increase security in the airports. They have not, however, made any rules about what happens after those doors close. Until they do that, we have made our own rules, and I want to share them with you. Once those doors close, we only have each other.

"The security has taken care of a threat like guns with the increased scanning, etc. Then we have the supposed bomb. If you have a bomb, there is no need to tell me or anyone else on this plane; you are already in control. So, for this flight, there are no bombs that exist on this plane.

"Now the threats that are left are things like plastics, wood, knives, and other weapons that can be made or things like that which can be used as weapons.

"Here is our plan and our rules. If someone or several people stand up and say they are hijacking this plane, I want you all to stand up together. Then take whatever you have available to you and throw it at them. Throw it at their faces and heads so they will have to raise their hands to protect themselves.

"The very best protection you have against knives are the pillows and blankets. Whoever is close to these people should then try to get a blanket over their head—then they won't be able to see. Once that is done, get them down and keep them there. Do not let them up. I will then land the plane at the closest place and we WILL take care of them.

"After all, there are usually only a few of them, and we are 200+ strong! We will not allow them to take over this plane.

"I find it interesting that the U.S. Constitution begins with the words 'We, the people'—that's who we are, THE people, and we will not be defeated."

With that, the passengers on the plane all began to applaud, people had tears in their eyes, and we began the trip toward the runway.

The flight attendant then began the safety

speech. One of the things she said is that we are all so busy and live our lives at such a fast pace. She asked that everyone turn to their neighbors on either side and introduce themselves, telling each other something about our families and children, show pictures, whatever. She said, "For today, we consider you family. We will treat you as such and ask that you do the same with us."

We learned that for the crew, this was their first flight since Tuesday's tragedies. It was a day that everyone leaned on each other and together everyone was stronger than any one person alone. It was quite an experience.

*

> *"It's very simple: There is only one requirement of any of us, and that is to be courageous. Because courage, as you might know, defines all other human behavior. And I believe, because I've done a little of this myself, pretending to be courageous is just as good as the real thing."*

—DAVID LETTERMAN, 9/17/2001

*

I was outside smoking a cigarette. That's right. Nothing spectacular, nothing great. I wasn't watching the news, I wasn't even paying attention to work. I was outside smoking a cigarette the day the world as we know it ended. All I was thinking about was going home on lunch, grabbing something to eat 'cause I missed breakfast, and smoking a cigarette.

Then a buddy came up to me and told me about the plane crashes, and I was so out of it that it didn't even register that it was an attack until he said that both happened within 15 minutes of each other. And that's when everything I knew came to a screeching halt. I stubbed the cigarette out, went back inside and listened to the radio, and told everyone I could.

About 30 minutes into just sitting there listening, we all looked at each other and knew what had to be done. We began to pack and prep our equipment. I'm in the Army, and I knew that this might happen . . . I never expected it to. I don't think any of us did. We train, we plan, but we never really think that, yes, this could happen. We're the United States of America, for Christ's sake!

But . . . it did happen. The world has changed, ladies and gentlemen, and I'm not sure what will come of it. I do know that, while most of the country is screaming for blood, we are demanding it. We're the protectors of this great country, and we failed.

The Doves of America were all killed on September 11, 2001 . . . and now there's nothing left but bloodthirsty Hawks.

*

> "Now the trumpet summons us again—not as a call to bear arms, though arms we need; not as a call to battle, though embattled we are; but a call to bear the burden of a long twilight struggle, year in and year out, 'rejoicing in hope, patient in tribulation,' a struggle against the common enemies of man: tyranny, poverty, disease and war itself."
>
> —JOHN F. KENNEDY,
> INAUGURAL ADDRESS, 1/20/1961

*

FROM AN AOL POST, 9/17/2001 3:41 PM
EASTERN DAYLIGHT TIME
SUBJECT: WE WILL SHOW THE WORLD

From the ruins of our buildings in New York and
Washington, D.C., and from the fields in Pennsylvania, where so many of our people paid the
ultimate price, will raise a cry for justice of such
magnitude that it will be heard even beyond our
own galaxy; we will not and we must not allow
those that perished to have died in vain.

The biggest tribute/memorial that we can erect
to them is the total and complete eradication of
terrorism in the world. Then and only then will we
have truly honored their memories; they deserve
nothing less.

*

*"We're building a strong coalition to go after these
perpetrators, but more broadly to go after terrorism
wherever we find it in the world."*

—SECRETARY OF STATE COLIN POWELL,
The New York Times 9/13/2001

*

"I believe that after the terrible tragedy of 11 September, the Vietnam syndrome is behind us. The public will support taking risks, and the armed forces are ready to do so."

—GENERAL WESLEY CLARK,
IN AN AOL CHAT 9/14/2001

FROM AN AOL POST, 9/17/2001 1:48 PM
EASTERN DAYLIGHT TIME
SUBJECT: WAIT . . .

We are not a patient people, yet we've been asked to wait . . . and wait we shall; for wait we must. There's an adage that states "Patience is a virtue . . ." and we are a virtuous people.

And so, we wait, collectively, while our trusted and empowered leadership forges an unprecedented alliance. We can take great solace in the sheer magnitude and breadth of our brethren, for it is global and approaching unanimity . . . I've also heard "A chain is only as strong as its weakest link . . ." Ironically, our chain has been galvanized and steeled by the very fires that sought to weaken it.

Phoenix-like, we rise from the ashes created by

an ignorance and prejudice that is impossible to comprehend. That extremism must be dealt with on the battlefield of tolerance . . . for, thankfully, we are a tolerant people.

We can, as we must, tolerate the waiting. We are an innumerable legion, taking comfort in our newly minted currency of singular purpose. We number many nations, cultures, and creeds . . . together seeking undeniable justice against a fanaticism that sought to engage the greatest nation on earth on the biased battlefield of intolerance. Knowledge is power, and we are mighty. Therefore, we wait.

But we wait in a collective multitude of faithful masses focused on the ultimate realization of triumphant and fundamental right. Prior to the awesome justice we are entitled to, I wish us all great peace and strength in our newly forged alliance . . . For somewhere in a distant land, perhaps, or possibly closer than we might expect . . . there is a person of such meager substance, yet capable of inspiring maniacal lambs to perpetrate suicidal atrocities . . . he is evil made tangible, and he waits, as we must . . . however, he waits ALONE.

"We will be patient, we will be focused, and we will be steadfast in our determination."

—PRESIDENT GEORGE W. BUSH,
Salon.com 9/17/2001

FROM AN AOL POST, 9/17/2001 1:34 AM
EASTERN DAYLIGHT TIME
SUBJECT: THE GREATEST GENERATION

When Tom Brokaw wrote *The Greatest Generation*, I remember thinking that the people of the 1940s rose to the occasion to defend the U.S.A. because they had to unite and get the job done. If Word War II had occurred in any another generation, I felt Americans of their day would be just as committed to freedom.

I know I was right, because our generation of 2001 has all the guts and heart of our grandparents. We will do all it takes to rid the earth of these cockroaches with faces that dare cross our borders and hurt our fellow citizens.

As happened in World War II, those terrorists have surely awakened the Sleeping Giant.

We are called the "United" States for a reason.

"We must go forward; but resolution, not rashness, must be the principle of our proceeding."

—JANE PORTER, *The Coquette*

FROM AN AOL POST, 9/16/2001 4:35 PM
EASTERN DAYLIGHT TIME
SUBJECT: HATE CANNOT BE FOUGHT
            WITH HATE!

What happened in New York and Washington, D.C. is a terrible tragedy.

Thousands of victims and their families have been violated. All of us have been violated. It is sad and makes us rightfully angry. We need to respond with force in order to keep this from happening again.

But visions of a quick "Mission Impossible" scenario are wishful thinking. It will be a long process. More Americans will probably die. Other innocents from other countries will be endangered as well. We are changed forever. Despite all of this, we have to keep free from hate and from retaliation and revenge for its own sake.

We are justified to fight back and must. Our

attitude is key—not to hate, but to know force is necessary. Without hate we will do what is necessary and no more. What that is exactly we don't know yet. We must be united in this.

If we allow hate to be our main emotion, we let the terrorists win. We become like them. With hate, we make mistakes. With hate, we turn on our own people who are different. American Arabs and Muslims who are equally appalled, who equally lost loved ones, who equally have the rights and dignity of everyone else, are not to blame.

Hate coupled with ignorance leads to stupid and equally terrorist activities. Ignorance that doesn't know a turbaned man is not even a Muslim. Ignorance that doesn't know the value Islam puts on human life. Hate caused the devastation.

Hate loses if we stick together and work together. Hate wins if we become a divided nation of those of us who are not Arab or Muslim and those of us who are. Then the will of the Terrorist is done and not the will of God, not the will that we say we believe as members of an open, diverse democracy.

"United we stand, divided we fall."

"The weak can never forgive. Forgiveness is the attribute of the strong."

—MAHATMA GANDHI

FROM AN AOL POST, 9/19/2001 4:42 AM
EASTERN DAYLIGHT TIME
SUBJECT: WE WILL RISE FROM THE RUBBLE

A poem written by the wife of a New York Police Department Lieutenant

We Will Rise from the Rubble
So many loved ones in Tower One and Two,
unaware of the horror terrorists could do.
Family, friends and rescuers alike,
left us so suddenly and took Father Mike.
For a shepherd they needed to guide
   them to heaven,
to be with their Lord and embrace their
   brethren.
More rescuers came to move steel, stone
   and wood,
they valiantly struggled to save those
   they could.

Day into night, night into day,
rescuers came from so far away.
"We the People" feel the loss and oh so
   much sorrow,
but we must stand together and think of
   tomorrow.
For there's no greater nation than the
   United States,
our homeland has been threatened and
   they just raised the stakes.
Terrorism is no game that we want to
   play,
but we cannot stand by for just one
   more day.
For those in our Nation whose loved
   ones they've lost,
there's no greater sacrifice, no greater
   cost.
May our prayers wrap around them like
   a blanket of love,
remember not what could have been but
   what was.
But if your loved ones knew our homeland's jeopardy,
would they lay down their lives to
   defend our country?

Now it's our turn to honor their precious memory,
so stand up and be counted by flying Old
Glory.
The terrorists will be found and they too
shall fall,
for the hurt and the pain that they
caused to us all.
Our soldiers are ready and we shall be too,
so be strong, America, for the red, white
and blue.

*

"Our skyline will rise again!"

—MAYOR RUDOLPH W. GIULIANI,
The New York Times 9/24/2001

*

FROM AN AOL POST, 9/18/2001 2:12 AM
EASTERN DAYLIGHT TIME
SUBJECT: PROUD TO BE AMERICAN

Things are slowly getting back to somewhat
normal, but every day we hear about someone

or someone's story of six degrees of separation. Each story hits closer to home. Who is missing, who is volunteering time/supplies; who are heroes and sadly who is scamming the public by taking advantage of everyone's emotional state . . .

The people who did this thought they would bring the USA to its knees, but what they don't get and understand is the SPIRIT of what AMERICA is all about. This has only mobilized us to do what is necessary to protect our way of life. This will not get us down. America will not let it happen!

As the wife of an Army Vietnam veteran and years later an Air Force veteran, the sister of a Naval Vietnam veteran, daughter of an Army WWII veteran, and niece of Army and Naval WWII veterans, I AM PROUD TO BE AN AMERICAN!

*

> *"We are going to rebuild. We need a living, breathing sign to the rest of the world that this is not going to crush us."*
>
> —NANCY PLOEGER, EXECUTIVE DIRECTOR OF THE MANHATTAN CHAMBER OF COM- MERCE, *Newsday* 9/13/2001

I wear a green uniform.

I was not born here on American soil, but I can only thank America for letting me have the chance to be able to grow up and live in peace and harmony. As I put on my uniform each morning, I think "Why did I join the armed forces?" And the answer is this: I gave up my own freedom so others may enjoy it.

I ask America—though we have lost loved ones, I ask that you do not hate. This is not what America believes in.

"Those who expect to reap the blessings of freedom must, like men, undergo the fatigue of supporting it."

—THOMAS PAINE, *The American Crisis #4*

FROM AN AOL POST, 9/23/2001 2:06 PM
EASTERN DAYLIGHT TIME
SUBJECT: I USED TO BE ANTI-WAR

I spent the late sixties and early seventies protest-
ing war. I spent the eighties and nineties, realizing freedom comes at a price, but secretly thankful
women can't be drafted. Now, in 2001, I realize that
if you're not part of the solution, you're part of the
problem.

If they need a 41-year-old RN, I'm going.

I wasn't lucky enough to have children, but I
want to help keep America free for the children
growing up now.

*

*"Is this not just another one of those moments when
America has been challenged, and will rise
again?"*

—RICHARD A. GRASSO, CHAIRMAN OF
THE NEW YORK STOCK EXCHANGE,
The New York Times 9/17/2001

*

FROM AN AOL POST, 9/13/2001 9:28 PM
EASTERN DAYLIGHT TIME
SUBJECT: 21ST-CENTURY MARTYRS

Ours is now the next "greatest generation" in the making. We will have to stand up to unimaginable horror and challenges from madmen whom we cannot easily identify.

Above all else, I know that we shall overcome because we are the seed of those brave and hardy souls that forged this country and protected it from all the demons of the past. We are of many colors, beliefs and also human frailties, but together we are an indomitable force.

We may all call God by a different name or no name at all . . . but each one of us has learned in this free society that God's true name is love.

*

"O Beautiful, for patriots' dream,
That sees beyond the years
The Alabaster cities gleam
Undimmed by human tears!"

—KATHARINE LEE BATES,
"AMERICA THE BEAUTIFUL"

TRANSFORMED

"Today, the world is not the same as it was yesterday. If we are the same as we were yesterday, then it is pure folly."

—RABBI YAAKOV PERLOW,
The New York Times 9/17/2001

❋

FROM AN AOL POST, 9/20/2001 3:16 PM
EASTERN DAYLIGHT TIME
SUBJECT: I AM CHANGED FOREVER

I thought that I was already appreciative of my life and the blessings and privileges we share as Americans. But this horrible tragedy has brought me to an even deeper understanding of all the wonderful joys of our life, here in the greatest nation on earth—I feel everything more deeply than ever.

My heart is broken for the families of the dead, missing, and injured. I mourn with them as if it were my own family, because we ARE all family. Yes, as a nation, we have our faults and we have made many tragic mistakes in the past .... but now I think I truly understand the incredible sacrifices made by our parents, grandparents, and forefathers to create this amazing country of America. I hope we all understand it more.

Most importantly, we must not let this newfound sense of purpose fade away as the weeks go by. We truly must all stick together. We must maintain our resolve. We must show the world that nothing can defeat us, no matter how horrible. We must care for each other, and improve our country and ourselves . . . for our children, for posterity, and especially as a tribute to all those who died, that they didn't die for nothing.

"One Nation, under God, with Liberty and Justice for all" . . . now more than ever.

FROM AN AOL POST, 9/20/2001 3:46 PM
EASTERN DAYLIGHT TIME
SUBJECT: RE: I AM CHANGED FOREVER

I agree with you one hundred and ten percent. Never before have I loved my husband and children more than when I watched those desperate souls jumping out of windows.

I think that was the hardest thing I have ever watched in my life, and I put myself in their shoes for an eternal second and just cried for three days straight. It has totally changed me and my life, although I'm not sure how.

I'm scared, not knowing if I'll wake up the next day or not. I know that I'll never look at my future or my children's future with the arrogance of knowing it will be there.

As those damn terrorists showed us all, you just never know!

"This was a tremendous warning to civilization that challenges us to mobilize, supremely, our sense of responsibility for this world."

—CZECH PRESIDENT VACLAV HAVEL,
The New York Times 9/12/2001

FROM AN AOL POST, 9/21/2001 12:04 AM
EASTERN DAYLIGHT TIME
SUBJECT: WHAT A DIFFERENCE A DAY
MAKES

On Monday we e-mailed jokes.
On Tuesday we did not.

On Monday we thought that we were secure.

On Tuesday we learned better.

On Monday we were talking about heroes as being athletes.

On Tuesday we relearned who our heroes are.

On Monday we were irritated that our rebate checks had not arrived.

On Tuesday we gave money away to people we had never met.

On Monday there were people fighting against praying in schools.

On Tuesday you would have been hard pressed to find a school where someone was not praying.

On Monday people argued with their kids about picking up their room.

On Tuesday the same people could not get home fast enough to hug their kids.

On Monday people were upset that they had to wait six minutes in a fast food drive-through line.

On Tuesday people didn't care about waiting up to six hours to give blood for the dying.

On Monday we waved flags signifying our cultural diversity.

On Tuesday we waved only the American flag.

On Monday there were people trying to separate each other by race, sex, color, and creed.

On Tuesday they were all holding hands.

On Monday we were men or women, black or white, old or young, rich or poor, gay or straight, Christian or non-Christian.

On Tuesday we were Americans.

On Monday politicians argued about budget surpluses.

On Tuesday, grief-stricken, they sang "God Bless America."

On Monday the president was going to Florida to read to children.

On Tuesday he returned to Washington to protect our children.

On Monday we had families.

On Tuesday we had orphans.

On Monday people went to work as usual.

On Tuesday they died.

On Monday people were fighting placement of the Ten Commandments on government property.

On Tuesday the same people all said "God help us all" while thinking "Thou shall not kill."

It is sadly ironic how it takes horrific events to place things into perspective, but it has. The lessons learned this week, the things we have taken for granted, the things that have been forgotten or overlooked . . . I hope they'll never be forgotten again.

*

"There is . . . throughout the world, a profound sense of solidarity; there is courage; there is a surging of the human spirit."

—BRITISH PRIME MINISTER TONY BLAIR,
AT A MEMORIAL SERVICE FOR BRITISH
VICTIMS OF THE NEW YORK TERRORIST
ATTACKS, AT ST. THOMAS CATHEDRAL,
9/21/2001

FROM AN AOL POST, 9/15/2001 2:02 AM
EASTERN DAYLIGHT TIME
SUBJECT: I THOUGHT I WAS A MAN!

My wife is sleeping. My girls are sleeping ... I know, because I just checked (something I have neglected to do for some time now because I have just been too busy). I will check on them more closely now, probably more frequently also.

My tears sting my eyes ... not MANLY, I know. My heart has shifted lately, and it goes out to the friends and families of those lost.

FROM AN AOL POST, 9/16/2001 6:25 PM
EASTERN DAYLIGHT TIME
SUBJECT: ALWAYS SAY "I LOVE YOU"

Despite the tragedies in the past week, I hope we as a nation have learned a valuable lesson—cherish the time we have with our loved ones. You could wake up tomorrow and never see them again. Never walk away angry. Don't fight over small things. Let's not take our families, friends, and significant others for granted. Respect each other and pray together.

And remember to always say "I love you." They may not be there when you come home.

***

"I do believe we shall continue to grow, to multiply, and prosper until we exhibit an association powerful, wise, and happy beyond what has yet been seen by men."

—THOMAS JEFFERSON,
LETTER TO JOHN ADAMS

***

FROM AN AOL POST, 9/15/2001 1:43 AM
EASTERN DAYLIGHT TIME
SUBJECT: I WANT TO BE AN AMERICAN

I am not an American citizen. I have been living in this country as a permanent resident for 16 years now, ever since I was 10 years old. For some reason I never took that last step to make it "official." I don't know why, maybe I thought that a little thing like that didn't make a difference.

Now I understand the difference that it will make. I see the people around me and the country I have grown to love and am proud to say is mine, and I know what it means to be an American. I know now that it is something that I want to be a part of. It is a beautiful country with wonderful people from all walks of life.

We take our freedoms for granted so often; now we know what it means to fight for them. I want to be a part of this great nation, I do not plan on ever leaving. I cannot wait to take my citizenship test and to get added to the list of people having the privilege to live in AMERICA.

*

"Since changes are going on any way, the great thing is to learn enough about them so that we will be able to lay hold of them and turn them in the direction of our desires. Conditions and events are neither to be fled from nor passively acquiesced in; they are to be utilized and directed."

—JOHN DEWEY, *Reconstruction in Philosophy*

*

FROM AN AOL POST, 9/16/2001 2:35 PM
EASTERN DAYLIGHT TIME
SUBJECT: POEM FOR THE VICTIMS AND
           THEIR FAMILIES

I'm not just an American,
my life was changed today.
I became a soldier,
in my own special way.

I couldn't stop the planes
or the terrorists taking our flights.
I wasn't there to comfort
the poor victims' screams and sights.

I wish I could have called out
for the buildings to be cleared,
but I wasn't in New York or Washington,
to comfort these people when they feared.

And when those brave souls on duty
didn't get home from work,
I didn't see their families
crying, shocked and hurt.

I didn't go through the rubble,

the fire or smoke to identify—
and didn't know who was who
or why they had to die.

But I'm not just an American,
and my life was changed today,
I became a soldier
in my own special way.

I put myself in their places
but couldn't imagine the strain.
I prayed for the victims' souls
and for their loved ones pain.

I listened to the tragic details,
too numb to really feel,
Then went out to give some blood
to help the wounded heal.

I woke my son the next morning,
only to hear him say,
"Nobody's going to school, Mom,
they were scared away."

I said, "You get up and go now,
even if you're the only one,

We're not going to show fear,
and no, they haven't won."

And as I put on my makeup,
my clothes, and working shoes,
a certain pride came over me,
one I never knew.

On the way out the door
I hung the flag at half mast,
put Red, White, and Blue on the car
and saw other flags that passed.

That certain message of liberty,
to fellow patriots we send,
symbolizing the freedom we earned
and the freedom we will surely defend.

We prayed along with the nation
with a request for God to save,
This beautiful nation of ours
and for bodies not yet in their grave.

Leaving work, emotions set in
as I drove home in the rain.
The tears began to fall

and I choked them back again.

Then the sun came out
forming a rainbow in the sky,
God's bright promise of hope
helped me not to cry.

Later we lit a candle,
and we prayed across this great land,
for the victims and their loved ones
because it's united we stand.

You see, we're not just Americans,
our lives were changed today.
We became soldiers
in our own special way.

*

"Our nation is united as never before. We are united not only in our grief, but also in our resolve to build a better world. At this service, we seek to summon what Abraham Lincoln called 'the better angels of our nature.'"

—JAMES EARL JONES, IN A STADIUM OF
HEROES, PRAYERS FOR THE FALLEN, *The New
York Times* 9/24/2001

FROM AN AOL POST, 9/16/2001 10:34 AM
EASTERN DAYLIGHT TIME
SUBJECT: WHILE WE MAY NEVER KNOW,
WE ARE SO THANKFUL

May the loss of thousands of lives on Tuesday forever remind us that the unthinkable can happen, and often does. May we resolve to move forward with a new respect for America and its great people. The victims of the disaster and the gallant men and women who lost their own lives attempting to save others will forever be a reminder of how precious life truly is.

*

"May we use this energy, may we use this unconditional spirit to go beyond this event so that we will become better people, more loving people, caring people, not only for the victims and the victims' families but also those who are impoverished in our nations, caught in the prisons of injustice and inequity."

—THE REVEREND EDWARD CORLEY,
MOUNT OLIVE BAPTIST CHURCH, MANHASSET, NEW YORK, *The New York Times* 9/17/2001

CONCERNED

HELPING

The September 11 terrorist attacks set in motion a chain of events—and emotions. Because almost everything about them was unprecedented, no one can say when we will return to "normal" or whether we'll have to adjust, over and over again, to a "new normal."

It's in the American tradition to reach out immediately to help those in need. That is noble. But because of the deep psychological wounds caused by the terrorist attacks, it is equally important for us to look inside and see if we are suffering—in our eagerness to give help, we may need to pause and, first, get help.

We have, therefore, divided this section into Giving Help and Getting Help—and because we suspect that we can be most useful to others if we are in good mental health ourselves, we start with ways to get help.

GETTING HELP FOR YOU
AND YOUR FAMILY

More than 1,000 American Red Cross chapters nationwide are prepared to work with the needs of your family surrounding this unprecedented tragedy. For the latest information regarding the Red Cross response and services the organization is providing, please visit *www.redcross.org.*

Childhelp USA® Hotline, 1-800-4-A-CHILD, offers assistance to children, families, and individuals who need help coping with the terrorist attacks.

The National Register of Health Service Providers in Psychology has pulled together a list of credentialed psychologists who have volunteered to offer healthcare services to the victims and their families. For the list, go to *www.nationalregister. com/reliefservices.html.*

The American Psychology Association gives advice on managing traumatic stress. Go to *www.apa.org/psychnet/coverage.html.*

The National Institute of Mental Health has a special section, Response to Terrorist Acts Against America. Go to *www.nimh.nih.gov/outline/ responseterrorism.cfm.*

GriefNet has e-mail support groups and an area where kids can help each other deal with their emotions. Go to *griefnet.org*.

Beliefnet enables you to find a local house of worship and provides a faith-by-faith guide for dealing with death and an online prayer circle for the victims of the terrorist attack. Go to *www.beliefnet.com*.

GIVING HELP

If you want to give money, many charities are addressing the aftermath of the terrorist attacks. For a good overview, go to *Helping.org* or *libertyunites.org*.

The following is a short list of organizations and charities.

NATIONAL ORGANIZATIONS

America's Second Harvest

America's Second Harvest's mission is to get food and water to hungry people. In the days after September 11, it was inundated with food and product donations. Now it needs cash donations to help move the disaster relief to the affected communities. For information about the America's Second Harvest Disaster Relief, go to *www.secondharvest.org/aboutash/disaster.html*.

American Red Cross

The American Red Cross, a humanitarian organization led by volunteers, guided by its Congressional Charter and the Fundamental Principles of the International Red Cross Movement, will provide relief to victims of disasters and help people prevent, prepare for, and respond to emergencies. For more information, please visit *www.redcross.org*.

AmeriCares

AmeriCares, the national and international disaster relief organization, has established a fund for the families of the New York City uniformed firefighters, police officers, and uniformed Port Authority employees who perished at the World Trade Center. For more information, visit *www.americares.org/InTheNews/Article.asp?id=161*.

Families of Freedom Scholarship Fund

The Families of Freedom Scholarship Fund has been created to provide education assistance for postsecondary study to financially needy children and spouses of those killed or permanently disabled as a result of the terrorist attacks. For more information, go to *www.familiesoffreedom.org*.

The Salvation Army

The Salvation Army has been serving meals to

emergency personnel each day of the rescue and recovery effort. Volunteers and supplies may again be needed. For more information, go to *www.salvationarmy-usaeast.org/disaster/index.htm.*

Save the Children

Save the Children trains counselors, teachers, parents, and volunteers to help children come to terms with these tragic events and to help communities to cope with traumas and crisis. For more information, visit *www.savethechildren.org/us_tragedy/fund.htm.*

The Tragedy Assistance Program for Survivors

The Tragedy Assistance Program for Survivors (TAPS) provides services to those who have been affected by the death of a loved one serving in the Armed Forces. The Department of Defense has directed the respective services to ensure all surviving family members are referred to TAPS for follow-up care and assistance. For more information about TAPS, visit their official website, *www.taps.org.*

NEW YORK CITY RELIEF EFFORTS

New York State World Trade Center Relief Fund

Governor George E. Pataki has established the World Trade Center Relief Fund for the benefit of the victims of the September 11, 2001, terrorist attacks. The purpose of the fund is to benefit all victims, both injured and deceased, and their families and dependants, including innocent civilians, firefighters, police officers, Port Authority police officers, emergency medical personnel and relief workers, and others impacted by the attacks. For more information go to *www.state.ny.us*.

September 11th Fund

The September 11th Fund was created by the United Way and The New York Community Trust to help with the immediate and longer-term needs of the victims and their families. For more information, go to *september11fund.org/epledge/ sept11.cfm*.

Twin Towers Fund

Mayor Rudolph W. Giuliani has established the Twin Towers Fund to coordinate the outpouring of support for the families of members of the New York City Fire Department and its Emergency Medical Services Command, the New York City Police Department, the Port Authority of New York and New Jersey, the New York State Office of Court Administration, and other government offices who lost their lives or were injured at the

World Trade Center. For information, go to *www.nyc.gov/html/em/twintowersfund.html.*

Survivors' Fund of the National Capital Region

The Survivors' Fund will focus on the long-term educational, health, income maintenance, and other needs of individual victims and their families in the metropolitan Washington, D.C., region. For more information, go to *www.cfncr.org.*

Police Organization Funds

New York City Police Foundation Heroes Fund

The New York City Police Foundation has established a special fund for police officers injured or killed in the World Trade Center relief effort. For more information, go to *www.nycpolicefoundation.kintera.org.*

New York Police and Fire Widows' and Children's Benefit Fund

The New York Police and Fire Widows' and Children's Benefit Fund assists the families of fallen New York City firefighters and police officers. For more information, go to *www.nypfwc.org.*

Firefighters' Funds

New York Fire Fighters 9-11 Disaster Relief Fund

The International Association of Fire Fighters (IAFF) will send financial assistance to the families of all fallen firefighters and EMS personnel. For more information, go to *daily.iaff.org/fund.htm*.

If You Want to Give Blood

In this period of uncertainty, the American Red Cross has a responsibility to assure blood availability regardless of any contingency including additional terrorist attacks in this country or U.S. military action. Donors are encouraged to set up an appointment to make a blood donation by calling 1-800-GIVE-LIFE or by visiting *www.redcross.org*.

ACKNOWLEDGMENTS

Thanks to Jonathan Sacks, president of America Online, for suggesting this book, and to Larry Kirshbaum and Maureen Egen of Warner Books for their willingness to publish it quickly and for the benefit of charity.

We also want to thank Jennifer Nessel for her help in researching, and Rose Hilliard for her help in assembling our content. Claire Zion gracefully shepherded the book through its accelerated publication process. Thanks also to the production team: John Kane, Jaime Putorti, Cecilia Marcon, David Honigsberg, Christopher Tinney, Rob Stauffer, Anna Maria Piluso, and Rebecca Springer.

For help in preparing our AOL content, we are grateful to an indefatigable team of researchers—Emily Heckman, Jod Kaftan, Jennifer Stroup, Sally

Swift, and Caroline Walker—who delved through some 60,000 message board posts. Anne Borsch eliminated obstacles as soon as they appeared. And we are deeply indebted to the AOL programmers, photo editors, community leaders, chat hosts, and others who worked around the clock for a week to create a vast online memorial and healing center.

Our greatest thanks go to the 31 million members of the AOL community, who shared their deepest feelings with us and made this book possible.